STRATEGIC MARKET RESEARCH

A Guide To Conducting Research That Drives Businesses

Third Edition

Anne E. Beall, PhD

STRATEGIC MARKET RESEARCH
A Guide To Conducting Research That Drives Businesses

Copyright © 2019 by Beall Research, Inc.

Cover Designed by Anne E. Beall

All images licensed through Shutterstock or owned by the author

ISBN: 9781731385178

For my colleagues at Beall Research

TABLE OF CONTENTS

Strategic Market Research 1

Table of Contents 2

List of Figures 3

List of Tables 4

Preface To Third Edition 5

Acknowledgments 7

Chapter 1: What's Wrong with Traditional Market Research? 9

Chapter 2: The Strategic-Question Approach to Market Research 13

Chapter 3: Using Hypotheses to Guide the Research 20

Chapter 4: Choosing the Right Method and Designing the Study 23

Chapter 5: Investigating Consumer Emotions in Qualitative and Quantitative Research 45

Chapter 6: Obtaining the Depth Required for Insight 58

Chapter 7: Reading the Hidden Communications of Research Respondents in Qualitative Research 64

Chapter 8: Analyzing Qualitative Data 80

Chapter 9: Analyzing Quantitative Data 89

Chapter 10: Interpreting Results and Going beyond the Data 101

Chapter 11: Common Pitfalls in Market Research 105

Conclusion 111

Anne E. Beall, Ph.D. 114

References 115

LIST OF FIGURES

Figure 1: Overview of Research Process 11

Figure 2: Decision Tree for Qualitative vs. Quantitative Research 25

Figure 3: Hierarchy for Project Designs 40

Figure 4: Intensity-Valence System for Emotions 47

Figure 5: Feelings About Self When Using Apple Brand 50

Figure 6: Imagery Associated with Hypothetical New Beverage 54

Figure 7: Simplified Example of Laddering Output 55

Figure 8: Framework for Explaining Chronic Overdrafting 82

Figure 9: Levinger's Model of Relationships 83

Figure 10: Brand 1 Word Cloud 84

Figure 11: Brand 2 Word Cloud 84

Figure 12: Brand 3 Word Cloud 85

Figure 13: Correspondence Analysis of Cellular Provider Plans 88

Figure 14: Segmentation That Views the Market in Two Different Ways 95

Figure 15: Example Simulator 96

Figure 16: Model for Major Company about What Predicted Purchasing 99

Figure 17: Tracking of Major Predictors over Time 99

Figure 18: Percentage of Invalid Responses Received vs. Length of Survey 107

LIST OF TABLES

Table 1: Examples of Good and Poor Research Questions 18
Table 2: Overview of Strategic-Question Approach 19
Table 3: Strategic Question and Hypotheses for Airline Project 22
Table 4: Strengths and Weaknesses of Different Research Methods...........................38
Table 5: Research Design for Win–Loss Study 41
Table 6: Research Design for Age by Geography..41
Table 7: Research Design for Age of Children by Area 42
Table 8: Confidence Intervals for Common Sample Sizes...43
Table 9: Research Design for Generation by Area of the United States 44
Table 10: Research Design for Type of Customers..44
Table 11: Analysis of Concepts and Keywords 86
Table 12: Linguistic Analysis 87
Table 13: Attributes That Have Greatest Impact on Likelihood to Return to Hotel and
Current Satisfaction..98
Table 14: Example Questions and Suggested Statistical Tool.....................................100

PREFACE TO THIRD EDITION

I first published this book in 2008 when I decided I wanted to share my approach to market research with people who buy and conduct it. I had started my business, Beall Research, 3 years earlier and I believed I was doing research a little differently. I never had any idea the book would sell as well as it did or that it would be used in colleges as a text book. It's now 2019 and my business is 16 years old. I still feel the same way: We conduct market research differently and I want to share that approach in the hopes that it will have an impact on someone who uses or conducts market research.

I truly love my industry, but to be honest, I never started out intending to do this for a living. It was my fascination with people that led me to study psychology in college and eventually to earn a PhD in social psychology from Yale University. While I was in graduate school, I became increasingly frustrated with the academic path in front of me. I had been trained to be an academic researcher and to teach college students, but I wanted to do more. I wanted to go into the "real world" and use my skills to help organizations. I wanted to make a difference. My career in market research has allowed me to make lasting, concrete changes in organizations for two decades. Market research is the study of how people think about and relate to brands, products, and services. When market research is done well, it helps companies respond intelligently to their markets and to offer products and services that people actually want and need. Market research has informed pasta-sauce companies that consumers want chunkier tomatoes; it has told car companies we want to listen to our iPods on our way to work, and it has even helped movie companies find the most appealing endings to films.

In the twenty-five years that I've been conducting market research, I've learned about many different businesses, worked on a variety of intellectually challenging problems, and seen the results of my research in the real world. I've seen new products launched that I was intimately involved with from the start, and I've watched ad campaigns that I initially tested (including a couple of Super Bowl commercials). I've seen people use products that would have never been designed if our research had not been conducted. I've seen companies become stronger and create more jobs because of the competitive edge our research gave them. And I know many of the products and services that we've researched have made a difference for the people who buy them.

It's my passion for this work that drove me to write this book. I believe in market research, and I want to give back to the industry that provided me with a way to make a living and the chance to make a difference. I wrote this book for people who buy or use market research and for those who conduct it. Some might say that it's not in my self-interest to share my approach with competitors, but I disagree. The better our industry becomes, the more we grow and the more value we will provide to our clients. Many companies use market research. This book applies equally to for-profit businesses and nonprofit organizations. We work with many different types of organizations, and I give many examples of these projects throughout this book.

This new edition has been updated to reflect new methods we've mastered, the new problems we've solved, and the new stories we have to tell. Yet no matter how much we've changed, the foundation remains the same. As an aside, I want to let you know that this is not a step-by-step instruction book that will help you write a survey from start to finish or to conduct a focus group if you've never done one before. It was never intended for that purpose. It provides a broad overview of things to think about (and what to avoid), how to design research effectively, how to measure emotions at a high level and how to think about presenting results so they make a difference.

I hope that you enjoy reading this book as much as I've enjoyed writing it.

-Anne E. Beall, Chicago

ACKNOWLEDGMENTS

There are many people who have helped me in my career and who have contributed greatly to the content of this book. My mentor at National Analysts, John Berrigan, taught me the basics of good market research and how to take research to a deeper, more consultative level. The group that I worked with at The Boston Consulting Group (BCG), particularly Jeannine Everett and Michael Silverstein, taught me how to use market research to shape the major strategies for an organization. While I was at BCG, my fellow researchers and I honed our interviewing skills, and I began to develop my thinking on reading nonverbal communication.

I want to thank the many clients I've worked with over the years and particularly since I began my company, Beall Research. My clients have pushed me as much as I've pushed them, and our partnership has been extraordinary. Many of the people I've worked with have suggested new ways of looking at issues or different ways to approach problems and they have used our research to created large changes in their organizations. I particularly want to thank Philip Dobbs, Phyllis DiMieri, Derick Prelle, Christine Barton, Scott Wagner, Andrew Low Ah Kee, Lori Iventosch-James, Chris Hsu, Allen Platek, Margo Borgione, Barbara Hulit, Kirsten Paust, Robert Smith, Carey Demos and Matt King. I've had longtime partnerships with many of you, and we have done some incredible work together. You are my heroes.

I also want to thank the many people at Beall Research who work with me every day, writing surveys, moderating interviews and focus groups, analyzing data, and writing reports. I want particularly to thank Tammy Corrigan, Steve Hudson, Christine Holt, Mark Geniesse, Gina Zuercher, Emma Sheehan, Cathy Noji, Philip Lukowicz, and Helen Argiroff-Flood. A special thank you goes to Mark Geniesse and Christine Holt for providing input to this edition of the book and also to Emma Sheehan who conducted the digital-listening analysis on cellular companies. I also want to thank the past and previous employees who will always be dear to me especially Peter Burgi, Matt Plishka, Matt Nestler and Elizabeth Henry.

Another group of people to whom I'm indebted are the respondents who have participated in my many projects. Because of your honesty and ability to share your thoughts and feelings, I have been able to garner tremendous insights.

CHAPTER 1: WHAT'S WRONG WITH TRADITIONAL MARKET RESEARCH?

Market research is a multibillion-dollar industry. In 2016, spending on market research in the United States was approximately $11.5 billion (Bowers & Brereton, 2017). That's a lot of money. Yet with all this spending on market research, it seems that many organizations still aren't getting work that is useful. Research buyers who spend thousands of dollars on market research don't always feel that they get the best value for their money; they don't get tremendous insights, and they don't acquire information that helps them make strategic decisions for their businesses. In short, they often have a lot of information but not many answers. Another complaint is that buyers sometimes feel that market research provides them with information that is so superficial that it tells them what they already know. The last complaint is that findings don't truly represent how and why buyers actually purchase products and services, which leads to poor business decisions. So, what is the problem?

Some critics of traditional market research say the techniques are to blame. They point out that focus groups can unduly influence research participants and cause respondents to espouse opinions that they don't really hold. Other critics claim that traditional market research tends to put forward rational explanations for human behavior, when people are more motivated by emotion than by rational reasoning. And yet other critics believe that human beings just can't tell us what they really think and feel and that one cannot determine the why behind consumer behavior. Some of these critics have turned to "big data" as a way to gain insight. Others have just tested things in the market and identified what works.

Other critics claim that it's the specific suppliers of market research who are to blame. Often, the more strategic thinkers sell the market-research study, and then the people who do the work lose their way with endless detail. What seemed like such a clear project in the beginning becomes myriad questions and a set of data that doesn't really say anything. Clients who are savvy in purchasing market research sometimes become allied with specific project managers who are able to take the initial questions and ensure they're answered at the end of a study. However, most individuals cannot be all things to all clients, so when techniques or questions change, this alliance may not be useful.

As someone who has been in market research since 1993, I don't believe that the problem is the techniques or the people. And I don't believe that consumers are unable to tell us how they behave and why. I believe there is validity in understanding consumer response before launching products, services and communications into the marketplace, and I believe "big data" can only go so far in explaining the reasons behind behavior. I say this as someone who has designed and executed hundreds of studies—both qualitative and quantitative—moderated hundreds of focus groups, conducted thousands of individual interviews, and fielded hundreds of surveys. I've also bought market research from top suppliers in the industry. Having seen the industry from both sides of the table, my observation is that the problem is how market research is designed, executed, and analyzed. Much market research comprises the gathering of information just for the sake of gathering it. It's not inspired, and it doesn't drive businesses to make decisions that will help them to compete.

I want to share my approach to conducting market research. My background combines academic training with real-world consulting. After completing my PhD at Yale University, I was hired by a consulting firm that taught academic researchers how to conduct business research. Eventually I worked at Boston Consulting Group, a major management-consulting firm, where I directed market research for its Chicago office. I now have my own firm, Beall Research, Inc. All of the research that I conduct is strategic in nature. Our research is different than much market research in terms of how we design it, how we obtain insight from respondents, and how we interpret what we learn. The purpose of this book is to share that approach.

The Strategic Approach

The strategic approach to market research is guided by five key principles. Following these principles ensures that results are actionable. These principles are

1. identifying the particular strategic questions that need to be answered;
2. ascertaining the hypotheses that need to be tested;
3. using the right research techniques to test hypotheses and answer the major strategic questions;
4. obtaining the depth required for insight;
5. going beyond the data to interpret the results and make strategic recommendations.

My experience is that good research projects include all of the above. In cases where the research breaks down, it's because one of the principles above is violated. These principles are relevant regardless of the organization that is commissioning the research. It doesn't matter if the organization is a Fortune 100 company or a small nonprofit association in the community.

Below is an overview of the typical process we use.

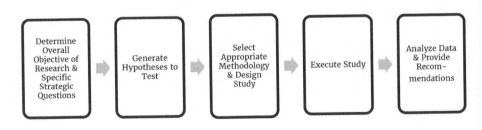

Figure 1: Overview of Research Process

How This Book Is Organized

I discuss each aspect of the research process and the principles of conducting actionable research in the following chapters. Each chapter builds on the previous one to show how the principles work together. Within each chapter, I highlight real examples of how I've used each principle to my advantage.

Chapter 2 is about the strategic question–based approach to market research, which is the foundation for designing a good project.

Chapter 3 is about developing hypotheses to test and using this approach throughout the project to gain the most insight.

Chapter 4 is about how to select the correct method. I discuss both qualitative and quantitative methods and explain the tradeoffs of each major one.

Chapter 5 is about how to investigate emotions in qualitative and quantitative research, which guide much of behavior.

Chapter 6 is about how to get the depth needed to gain useful insights that answer strategic questions.

Chapter 7 is about how to read the nonverbal communications of research respondents. Often, these nonverbal behaviors tell us volumes about what people think and feel.

Chapter 8 is about how to analyze qualitative data and some techniques that we find helpful.

Chapter 9 discusses how to analyze quantitative data and the major types of statistical analyses one can use to address certain questions.

Chapter 10 is about how to interpret findings from a market-research study; it provides guidelines for how to go beyond the data to help an organization.

Chapter 11 is about some of the common pitfalls that occur in market research. I've seen all of them, and they're easy to avoid if you know them in advance.

CHAPTER 2: THE STRATEGIC-QUESTION APPROACH TO MARKET RESEARCH

I f there is one thing that can make the difference between excellent and poor market research, it's the nature of the question that's being asked. My experience is that the best projects tend to be ones in which a very specific question with strategic significance for an organization is answered. Unfortunately, many research projects tend to have many vague questions that the organization wants to answer. Often, the result of all these questions is a long discussion guide (in the case of qualitative research), or in the case of quantitative work, a long survey. This approach tends to reveal a large amount of information across a variety of topics, but it tends to have little depth.

I once did some work for a dental-supply company that had done very little research about its customers: dentists all over the country. Because the company had done so little market research, the client wanted to know almost everything about the customers. The company wanted to know how dentists viewed their products, how they made decisions, how often they saw representatives from competitors, what they regarded as the strengths and weaknesses of the company's products, how they felt about competitor sales reps, what they thought about their logo and so on. The list was endless. We ended up with a long discussion guide for individual interviews with dentists all over the country. At the end of this study, we knew a little about a lot of things. The client was disappointed. He claimed that he already knew much of what we had learned and that he had gained few strategic insights about what to do with his company. That experience was a valuable lesson for me.

What I learned was that trying to answer many questions is often less valuable than answering one or two major questions. Answering one or two well-chosen questions allows one to obtain the depth required to provide strong, actionable recommendations. I like to compare the dental-supply company with a nonprofit association that approached me about doing market research to determine if it would make sense to change its name. The question was clear and straightforward. Some of their members thought the name was old-fashioned and that it gave an inaccurate perception of the association. I suggested interviewing members about their perceptions of the association, their perceptions of the name, whether they thought the name should be changed, and if so, what a new name should convey. The results of this research indicated that the association should keep its name but should change its logo and marketing materials. The clients were pleased with the study because it gave them clear answers to a major question and it provided strategic direction for them.

So, clearly, having a few good questions is preferable to having many questions. Sometimes, though, one question can be a poor question. Whenever clients approach me about doing research for them, I always ask what their objective is in conducting this work. On many occasions, people will tell me that their company wants to "understand our customers better," "figure out what's important to customers," or "identify how to sell more of our products and services." All of these questions are very vague, and they presume a number of questions underneath each one. "Understanding our customers better" is not an objective that can be clearly translated into a market-research project. Every organization wants to understand its customers or clients. It's the specifics of what an organization wants to understand that form the basis of a good question.

Assessing Research Questions

So, what makes a good question? A good question leads to a specific answer that provides a clear direction for the organization. A good way to assess potential research questions is to use the following evaluation criteria:

Is there a major **strategic objective** that the organization is trying to achieve?
- Are they trying to grow market share?
- Are they trying to identify a new market to enter?
- Are they thinking about changing a current product or service?

      o   Are they thinking of launching a new product/service?

Is there a **clear, strategic question** that the organization needs to answer to address this objective?

- What specific changes to our product would lead to increased purchasing?
- How do current customers view our potential new product/service idea?
- What are the reasons market share has declined?

Are there **specific strategic sub-questions** that need to be answered in order to fully address the major strategic question?

- For example, the question "What are the reasons market share has declined?" actually has some sub-questions, such as:
  - o Are people dissatisfied with our product/service?
  - o Do they prefer a competitor's offering over ours?
- Similarly, the question "What specific changes to our product would lead to increased purchasing?" comprises the following questions:
  - o If we changed X, would that increase purchasing or usage?
  - o If we added Y, would that increase purchasing or usage?
- The question, how do current customers view our new potential product/service idea also has sub-questions:
  - o Do current customers like the new product/service idea?
  - o Would they purchase it at X price?
  - o How many would they buy over a certain period of time?

And most importantly, if the organization knew this information, would they take **specific actions** as a result?

- What would the company do if they knew this information?

If you can answer yes to all the criteria above, then you have an excellent strategic question. See table 1 for some examples of good and poor research questions.

In many cases, organizations don't approach us with excellent questions. Our job is to help them think through their objectives and to arrive at questions that can be turned into good research designs. We strive to meet the criteria discussed above. In situations where clients have a vague question or a conglomeration of questions, we help them to identify the strategic questions. The approach that we use is to ask them a series of questions that will illuminate the major issues. We will ask questions such as:

- Is there a current issue or problem that is motivating the commission of this research?
- What is the major objective of this study?
- Which person or department is driving this research?

- What is the reason you want to conduct research? What are some of the *specific* things your organization wants to understand?
- If you had to prioritize the set of things you want to know, what are the first, second, and third things you would want to learn?
- What actions would your organization take as a result of knowing this information?

We have found that, as clients begin to think about these questions, their vague, conglomerated questions become clearer. A bunch of disjointed questions becomes one or more strategic questions with several specific sub-questions

For example, clients may say that they want to understand their customers better so they can sell more of their housecleaning services. After a discussion, we may find that they had placed banner ads on websites to try to win new customers. These ads didn't bring in new business, and they want to understand why. The strategic objective of "We want to sell more housecleaning services" has illuminated the following questions: 1) Do people respond to banner ads about housecleaning services? 2) If they do respond to banner ads, what was the problem with these recent ads—why didn't they work? 3) If people don't respond to ads, how do they find housecleaning services? 4) What criteria do people use in evaluating potential housecleaning services—in other words, what do people want to know before they will call to inquire about a housecleaning service? Thus, the strategic question is "What medium and what communications should we use to win new customers?" The specific questions that were just outlined fall under this strategic query.

After defining the major questions for an organization, we always ask how they would use the information. We ask:

- What would the organization do if it knew this information?
- What specific decisions would the organization make in response to this research?
- What can the organization realistically change or do in response to the results from this project?

This information is critical to understanding some of the specifics of what organizations need to know. In the housecleaning example, we might learn that as a result of this project, this business will determine which marketing vehicles to use and how much money to allocate. Thus, we would want to understand where these customers go when looking for information on housecleaners. This business might also want to know what was positive or negative about the recent ad it placed. For this project, we would want potential customers to look at the ad and tell us what the ad conveys to them and the major reasons they would or wouldn't call in response to it.

When you go through this process and help people to reframe their research questions, what begins as one type of project can evolve into a totally different one. I once worked with a large organization that provides educational materials to instructors all over the country. It had changed some of its materials and wanted to have instructors review all of these changes and give them feedback. I reviewed their new materials and couldn't see any major differences from their earlier ones. I asked the clients what 'they ultimately wanted to accomplish; they explained that they believed the materials were improved and they wanted to make sure instructors would not reject them. Their initial question changed from one about how instructors feel about the new materials to "How do we communicate the changes in our materials to instructors?" The specific questions that we needed to answer were: 1) Do instructors notice the changes, and if they do, which ones do they notice? 2) How do they feel about these changes—are they perceived as improvements or not? 3) What do instructors want to know about these changes in order to feel positively about them? In other words, what justification do they need to understand these changes? Because we reframed the question, we ended up providing a great deal of value to this organization. We turned a somewhat trivial project into one where the information was used to create a communication strategy for the new course materials.

See table 2 for an example of this approach laid out very simply. This hypothetical example is for an airline that was having trouble retaining current customers. We outlined the major objective, the strategic questions that could help reach this objective, and the actions that could be taken as a result of these questions being answered.

Poor Strategic Question	Good Strategic Question
What is important to customers?	What specific needs does this product or service fulfill?
How is our product perceived compared to those of competitors?	How do customers perceive the features of our product compared to the features of our competitor's product? Do customers value the major feature that differentiates our product from the competition? Would this product replace usage of other similar products in the marketplace?
How do customers make decisions when purchasing this service?	What are the key criteria that people use when selecting this service? What 2–3 criteria are the most important?
What do customers think about this potential new product?	How likely would customers be to purchase this product with these specific features at this particular price?
What do customers think about this new service?	What do customers specifically like and dislike about this service? What are the unmet needs this service would fulfill?

Table 1: Examples of Good and Poor Research Questions

Business Issue	Current customers are not being retained. Many customers use the airline 1–2 times and then use competitors.
Strategic Objective	We want to retain more of our current customers.
Major Strategic Question	What are the major reasons that customers don't remain loyal after using our airline?
Specific Sub-questions to Answer Strategic Question	How do customers experience our airline? What do they like/dislike about the experience? What are the major reasons they are using competitors instead? What specific parts of the experience might lead to greater loyalty? Would a loyalty program increase customer retention?
Potential Actions	Changes to customer experience of airline Design of loyalty program

Table 2: Overview of Strategic-Question Approach

CHAPTER 3: USING HYPOTHESES TO GUIDE THE RESEARCH

O nce we know the overarching business issue, the major strategic question, and associated sub questions, we want to think about any hypotheses that should be tested in the research. Hypotheses are important because they suggest some of the current thinking within an organization. They can provide some insight into what people believe would remedy a problem or what would make a product or service successful. For example, we might learn that one group believes that pricing is the major reason why customers are going to other airlines and that people just don't have "loyalty" to airlines. They further believe that a loyalty program that provides discount pricing after a certain amount of usage would be the answer.

These hypotheses can provide clear direction to the research, which makes it more relevant to the organization commissioning it and more likely to drive actual results. I believe that this area is one of the major ones where market research "drops the ball" and causes frustration for many end users. They have specific ideas about why something is occurring or how it can be changed, and the research never supports or refutes their ideas. End users are left disappointed because a specific question was not asked that would have provided them with the information they needed.

Clients are sometimes loath to provide us with hypotheses that we can use for the research. "We don't know the answers to these questions; that's why we hired you" is sometimes what we hear them say. We once had a client who wanted to change the name of a nonprofit firm, and they wanted to know how people felt about the name. They hypothesized that people didn't like the current name and that they would prefer another name they had already selected. We put questions in the survey about how people perceived the name and whether they preferred a different name or not. The client promptly removed these questions and claimed that they could deduce whether the name was problematic or not. If they made the decision to change the name, it was certainly based on their own opinions and not from the research.

In cases where clients find hypotheses hard to generate, we ask them to fill out the template below (see table 3). In the example below, we return to the airline with trouble retaining customers. We identify the major strategic sub-questions and generate potential answers (hypotheses) for these questions.

S1: How do customers experience our airline?
S2: What do they like/dislike about the experience?
S3: What are the major reasons they are using competitors instead?
S4: What specific parts of the experience might lead to greater loyalty?
S5: Would a loyalty program impact retention?

For each strategic sub-question, we generate one or more hypotheses:

S1: How do customers experience our airline?

- H1: Customers are somewhat satisfied with our airline—neither very satisfied nor very dissatisfied.

S2: What do they like/dislike about the experience?

- H2: They like the flying experience but find the airport/gate experience problematic.

S3: What are the major reasons they are using competitors instead?

- H3: They use competitors' airlines because the pricing is better and the experience is the same.

S4: What specific parts of the experience might lead to greater loyalty?

- H4: If we had better pricing, they might use us more, and if we had more on-time flights, they might be more loyal.

S5: Would a loyalty program impact retention?

- H5: A loyalty program that offered better pricing might increase retention.

With this information, we now have something that we can really use to design the survey or write the discussion guide for an interview or focus group. We know not only the kind of answers our clients need but also what kind of data they would actually use.

Once we have the general hypotheses, it's useful to have a further conversation about some of the specifics of each hypothesis. For example, we would ask our clients why customers are neither satisfied nor dissatisfied with the airline. Getting further clarification can provide the researcher with the grounding in the subject, which will help with the project. See table 3 for a template that can be used to get further information about each major hypothesis.

As the project progresses, we often are able to offer provisional answers to clients' hypotheses while we come up with hypotheses of our own. Imagine that we've been conducting interviews with two kinds of customers of the troubled airline: those who used the airline once and never used it again and those who continued to use it. The client hypothesized that customers are neither very satisfied nor very dissatisfied with the experience. After interviewing many customers, we decide that there is little evidence for that hypothesis. Instead, we're finding that a minority of customers are very dissatisfied and many customers are somewhat satisfied. As a result of this new information, we may hypothesize that there are different groups in the market who have different expectations of flying. At this point, if we're doing interviews or focus groups, we may want to probe on what flyers' expectations are and whether they were met or not. Or if we're looking at quantitative data, we may want to see what "satisfaction groups" seem to be emerging in the data and how they differ.

Once we have a good overview of the business issue, the major strategic question, sub-questions, and the major hypotheses, we want to begin thinking about the best way to conduct this research. In the next chapter, we provide an overview of the different methods and the positive and negative aspects of each one.

Strategic Question	What are the major reasons that customers don't remain loyal after using our airline?
Specific Sub-questions to Answer Strategic Question	S1: How do customers experience our airline? S2: What do they like/dislike about the experience? S3: What are the major reasons they are using competitors instead? S4: What specific parts of the experience might lead to greater loyalty? S5: Would a loyalty program impact retention?
Potential Hypotheses	H1: Customers are somewhat satisfied with our airline—neither very satisfied nor very dissatisfied. H2: They like the flying experience but find the airport/gate experience problematic. H3: They use competitors' airlines because the pricing is better and the experience is the same. H4: If we had better pricing, they might use us more, and if we had more on-time flights, they might be more loyal. H5: A loyalty program that offered better pricing might increase retention.

Table 3: Strategic Question and Hypotheses for Airline Project

CHAPTER 4: CHOOSING THE RIGHT METHOD AND DESIGNING THE STUDY

All research methods have pros and cons, and there are many ways to conduct a study. Market researchers sometimes criticize one another for using specific methods while espousing the strengths of their own. I always find these conversations amusing because research design is both an art and a science. Generally, with qualitative research, an excellent moderator who is using a research method that she is comfortable with will end up providing useful information. In quantitative research, a thoughtful, well-worded survey covering the major issues will deliver tremendous value. In many cases, the shortcomings of research tend to be the result of not taking a strategic-question approach to the problem and not understanding the issues that are important to the organization, which was just discussed in chapter 2.

In this chapter, I talk about the major market research methods available and some of the tradeoffs of using each one. The objective of this discussion is to acquaint you with some excellent uses for each method and some of the pitfalls of each approach. It's not meant to be an exhaustive summary of every potential methodology with all possible pros and cons. However, before considering each method, one has to decide whether to conduct qualitative or quantitative research.

Qualitative or Quantitative Research?

Qualitative research methods all collect qualitative data—thoughts, feelings, usage patterns, and so on. Examples of this method include focus groups, individual interviews, and observational research. Quantitative research comprises methods in which you gather numeric data of some type and the sample sizes are large enough to do statistical analyses (typically from hundreds to thousands of respondents). Examples include internet surveys, telephone surveys, and in-person intercept surveys.

So, when do you do qualitative versus quantitative research? The straightforward answer is that when you want to collect numeric data, quantitative research is the way to go. That answer isn't necessarily correct. Often, people don't know what kind of data they need, and having information in numeric form isn't as important as having good answers. Typically, we suggest doing qualitative research if little or no work has been done on the topic and if the project is somewhat exploratory. Qualitative work allows us to explore all the potential thoughts, feelings, and behaviors of a particular group of people. It's only when we understand all of these things that we can confidently measure them in a survey. Qualitative work also provides us with an opportunity to generate additional hypotheses that we can test in quantitative work. Thus, our quantitative research is well informed by our qualitative work.

Below is a decision tree you can use to determine whether you should use qualitative or quantitative research. Once you identify the questions you want to answer and what you already know, you can begin to think about how much precision you need in your answer. For example, if you want to know whether to launch a new product, know very little about the market and need a precise number, you'll need to do a qualitative-quantitative methodology. It's also important to think about the potential risk involved in doing (or not doing) research. If a decision will require several million dollars of investment or beating a competitor to market in order to gain market share, there will be a bias toward designing research that is quantitative in nature and that has a small margin of error.

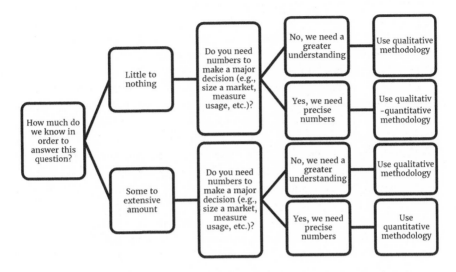

Figure 2: Decision Tree for Qualitative vs. Quantitative Research

Qualitative Methods

There are numerous qualitative methods that can be used. We now explore some of those most commonly used and their major advantages and disadvantages.

Focus Groups, Minigroups, and Triads

Focus groups, which are group discussions moderated by a facilitator, are a common qualitative method. The major advantage of focus groups is that you can hear from numerous people in a small amount of time and get a broad overview of thoughts, feelings, and behaviors, particularly if you talk with many different types of people. Another advantage is that you can use the group dynamic to explore issues in a way that would be more difficult with an individual. The major disadvantage of focus groups is that the group dynamic can sometimes get in the way of collecting individual's thoughts and feelings, especially if respondents aren't proud of these opinions. I will discuss pros and cons of this approach in detail.

The major advantage of focus groups is that you can use the group dynamic to unearth things that are difficult to obtain from individuals. Groups can create an atmosphere of trust and disclosure and an easy interchange of ideas. For example, some of the work that we've done in the past is for clinical trials. All medications must be tested in clinical trials to be approved by the FDA. Organizations that run clinical trials communicate effectively with people who participate in clinical trials, so they want to understand what motivates them to participate in them. Some people want to make a contribution to the world, and others want to try a new treatment because they're dissatisfied with their current one. These conversations can be very emotional. It's often difficult for one person to articulate some of these deep-seated feelings and what his or her participation might mean to him or her. Usually, one person begins to explain these feelings and another one will expand on these thoughts and further articulate them. Other group members will begin to add their thoughts to the subject, and as a result of this group process, we will understand something that's complicated.

The group setting also allows members to stimulate one another's thinking. At my company, we use focus groups to generate broad lists of thoughts, feelings, and behaviors. For example, in work for a retail store, we generated all the words that come to mind when people hear that store's name. Respondents said the words that came to mind, and these words sparked new words in response. The list became long, and several key themes emerged. These themes were then analyzed to describe this retail brand. We also do similar exercises with respondents about all the major uses they have for a particular product—the reasons they use the product and when they tend to use it. Getting ideas for all of these uses helps us determine when and why things are used. We also use focus groups to generate creative ideas. Sometimes we use creative consumers—respondents who have been specially trained to use their creativity to help businesses—or sometimes we just have respondents think about all the unique ways to use or think about something.

All is not rosy with focus groups, however. Sometimes, people are unduly influenced by other respondents, particularly ones with dominant personalities. If a moderator doesn't maintain control of the discussion, a respondent with a strong personality can unduly influence a group, and it can limit others from sharing their point of view. At the end of the group, one is unsure what the other respondents were actually thinking. Another problem is that people may be less likely to divulge what they really think and do in a group because they're actively managing the impression they give to others in this setting. The result could be a focus group in which people are telling you what they think they should say rather than what they actually do or think. These criticisms are all valid. Expert moderators generally have ways of creating an atmosphere for honest disclosure and have ways of handling these types of problems. We also have ways of judging whether people are actively managing how they come across rather than revealing what's really going on in their lives.

One of the major issues with focus groups is something called *group polarization*. Interestingly, groups tend to intensify their members' opinions if they all share a particular viewpoint. Thus, if all the people in a focus group tend to be positively predisposed toward a particular politician before the discussion, they will be even more positive about this person after it. Apparently, the group members reinforce one another's ideas and encourage stronger attitudes. This effect has been found in numerous research studies across many different people (Myers 2002). Group polarization can have a tremendous impact on how you interpret focus-group findings because you can misread a group's enthusiasm for or aversion to a product. You may believe that this product will be a hit (or a tremendous bomb) if you don't factor in the polarization effect. Good moderators have ways of creating dissension in groups and encouraging other viewpoints to address this effect. However, group polarization is sometimes inescapable.

Over the course of twenty years, I've become increasingly enamored of minigroups (four to five people per group) and triads (three people per group). These types of focus groups allow for a greater degree of depth with each person than the traditional eight- to ten-person group, and they allow more intimate disclosures. This method is one that we've become very comfortable using because it balances breadth and depth while using the group dynamic. The key downside here is cost in time and money. This method is not as efficient as a larger focus group and takes more time as a result. It ultimately costs more per respondent as well.

Individual Interviews—In the Home, at Work, or in a Facility

Individual interviews, as the name implies, involve talking to only one person. Thus, projects with individual interviews tend to involve fewer total respondents than focus-group projects. However, these interviews allow us to explore individual motivations and behaviors in great detail and to piece together the various influences on behavior. We use these interviews to elicit what is important in the abstract and then to have people give us stories of their experiences buying or using a product or service. These stories often tell us about all the actual influences on behavior, and we can analyze these stories to see if there are common themes. We can also compare these stories to the abstract reasons that people give us about what's important to them. Sometimes, what people say is important is not actually borne out in their examples. For example, in some individual interviews, consumers told us that price is an important factor in their decision to purchase household goods. However, their stories told us otherwise

Where we conduct individual interviews varies. We prefer to go to people's homes or workplaces if we believe that understanding these environments is important for that product or service. Respondents' homes and workplaces can reveal important aspects about how they live and work. These environments can also reveal what is important to people. In a recent project for an apparel company, we went to teens' homes to understand the clothing that is important to them and to see how clothing creates part of their identity. We asked teens to bring out some of their favorite clothing. Some of the teens took us into their rooms to get their clothing, and we were able to see how these teenagers arranged their spaces, what they put on their walls, and how they defined themselves. We gained much more insight about these teens as a result of using this method. We also use this method if we have trouble getting respondents to come to a facility. For example, when we interview executives, we sometimes have difficulty getting them to come to our locations, so we go to their workplaces.

The major drawback of individual interviews is the amount of time one needs to conduct them. Our interviews are typically at least one hour long. When we do in-home or at-work interviews, the amount of time we expend on travel and interviewing can be as much as three hours for each person. In cases where we don't believe that going to someone's home or workplace is useful, we will do individual interviews in a facility. Another drawback is that these interviews involve so much depth with each person that one can sometimes feel, at the end of ten interviews, that there are ten different stories with no particular pattern in the results. As a result, we tend to do ten interviews for each customer group, and then we analyze the group of interviews for consistent patterns.

In-Depth Telephone Interviews

In situations where we're interviewing a small number of people who are spread across a wide geography, it makes sense to do an in-depth interview that uses a webcam using programs such as Skype. The advantage of this method is that we can interview people around the world and be able to see their faces. For example, some of the studies we conduct are with business decision makers who are located all over the United States. Even if we could interview them in a facility or at their workplaces, they have a tendency to be very busy and to cancel appointments at the last minute. In these situations, it makes sense to conduct an in-depth telephone interview; we can schedule it at the person's convenience, we don't need to travel to fifteen different cities, and, if participants cancel at the last minute, we haven't absorbed huge travel costs.

In addition to these obvious advantages, in-depth telephone interviews can be very useful for sensitive subjects that people may be uncomfortable discussing in person. I have a colleague who only does in-depth telephone interviews because he's convinced that people disclose more over the telephone with him than when they're with him in person. I think it depends on the topic that you're discussing. If you're talking about something that's highly personal and would benefit from the anonymity of the telephone, it can be a very useful method. However, if you set the right atmosphere for disclosure, an in-person interview can accomplish the same things as a telephone interview.

One disadvantage is that you may not always have the ability to see the persons' face, which means that a whole host of nonverbal cues are unavailable to you. I talk about reading the hidden communications of research respondents and the type of information you can glean from people by their body language in an upcoming chapter. When someone doesn't want to do a webcam interview there is no option to observe this person's body language. The other disadvantage is that people have a tendency to multitask while you're interviewing them if they can't be seen. People answer e-mails, surf the internet, and sometimes eat during interviews. Obviously, you don't always have respondents' full attention.

Shop-Alongs

Shop-alongs are shopping trips that we make with respondents. We use this method when we want to understand the effect that a retail environment has on a person. In a group discussion or individual interview, respondents will tell you to the best of their knowledge how stores influence their behavior, but often they don't really know how they shop in stores and what induces them to buy certain items. Because we can't expect human beings to have perfect insight into themselves, we go shopping with respondents to see the effects of retail environments, sales associates, and brands on consumer behavior for ourselves.

When I first started my business, I received a call from a major bedding manufacturing company that wanted to do focus groups to understand what is important to consumers when buying its product. I had a hunch that people didn't always know what they want when it comes to this product because it was a fairly infrequent purchase, and I suspected that the retail environment has a large influence on shopper behavior. I recommended doing shop-alongs to ascertain the impact of the store on customers. They were a little leery about this method, but they were intrigued, and we started doing shop-alongs. The results were very illuminating. Customers were tremendously influenced by the salespeople and by the environment in which they were shopping. Often, they would walk in with a certain brand and specific product in mind and then would buy something completely different. They changed their minds because the sales associate would educate them about new technology or encourage them to buy a different product and brand. The results helped to change how salespeople were trained and how this product was sold in major stores.

I am a tremendous proponent of shop-alongs, but only when you need to understand how stores influence customers and when you want to learn how customers shop for certain products. Shop-alongs are not a great source for insight about why products are preferred or how people use them. Typically, the output of shop-alongs is an overview of the shopping process and what is effective or ineffective in a retail environment for a particular category. The major disadvantage of this method is that it can be time-consuming and the researcher's presence can sometimes alter the respondent's behavior. We try, however, to create as normal an interaction as possible and have gleaned a tremendous amount of insight from this method.

Observation

Another useful method is observation. We have learned a great deal from just watching customers use things that they buy. In a study that we did for a food manufacturer, I observed how people store and prepare food when they have young children. When you look at what they buy and store in their pantries, you get a better understanding of what really matters. I learned that often what people tell you about their desire for nutritious foods is not borne out when you look at the foods they cook and serve. Although mothers will say that they only care about serving their children nutritious food, it appears that getting young children to eat with as little fuss as possible at the table may be more important.

Sometimes, before doing qualitative research on a topic, I will observe as many people as possible to understand customer behavior. In a study that on greeting cards, we spent time watching people shop for greeting cards at local stores. We noticed that there were several segments of greeting card shoppers and that they approached the cards quite differently. As a result of watching people closely, we could see that there was clearly a group that was highly involved with the category, and they enjoyed the selection process. At the other end of the spectrum were people who wanted to pick up a card as quickly as possible and get out. There were several other segments in between. Knowing these segments helped us to understand how to structure the qualitative research and to sample each of these groups.

Online Discussion Forums and Online Focus Groups

As our communication becomes more reliant on electronic media, the research community has fully embraced online methods such as discussion forums and online focus groups. With discussion forums, a moderator posts a question and respondents post their answers online over the course of several days when it's convenient for them. Online focus groups occur over the course of two hours and are very similar to a traditional focus group except that they occur via webcam online.

We have successfully used online discussion forums and online focus groups in several situations. We have found they're useful when the respondents are not geographically close enough to have a focus group. We've also found them useful when we want to have a discussion among a national sample of people. For example, we did a study with instructors who were located all over the country. There were not enough of them in several geographic locations to conduct the number of focus groups that we wanted, so we did an online discussion forum with people all across the United States. We then did two to three focus groups in two major cities where there were enough people to recruit in-person focus groups.

One advantage of these methods is that sometimes people feel more comfortable interacting online than they do in person. Individuals in their 20's and 30's tend to be particularly comfortable communicating in this way because they spend a lot of time interacting electronically. Older respondents may find this anonymity particularly comfortable, especially if they are discussing highly personal or embarrassing topics. One of my colleagues just did a study in which she was discussing female sanitary supplies with women. The online discussion forum proved to be the perfect method for having this sensitive discussion.

The major disadvantage of these methods is that they don't occur in person, so you can't observe respondents' nonverbal communication. Even worse than not being able to see respondents' body language is the possibility that respondents can lie in an online environment and pretend to be someone they're not. Electronic communications offer people the opportunity to role-play and to assume identities that aren't real. There is often no way to tell if that's happening. Online focus groups can also be challenging because of the software—there can be delays between asking and answering questions, everyone is seen simultaneously and the conversation doesn't feel like a group dynamic and as a result feels unnatural. This method can sometimes be more like several one-on-one interviews where each person answers each question when called upon.

The issue of posing online is not insignificant and I have a colleague in Australia who had an experience with that. She was conducting a study with women who had just had a child. The study involved an online discussion forum with the mothers within a month after they had given birth. The online discussion was followed with an in-home interview, where the researcher took a picture of the new baby and mother and discussed various baby products. My colleague went to one respondent's house to conduct the interview. The husband answered the door and told her that the respondent was not home and had not given birth within the past twenty years. My colleague was amazed that the respondent had been posing as a new mother for several months of this study. In future studies she has found other ways to confirm that a person is actually a new mother.

Mobile-Qualitative Methods

When one wants to understand the reaction of a person to a specific situation at a specific time, there are useful qualitative methods using cell phones to capture pictures, short surveys, and texts about reactions to products/services. For example, if you want to understand what's important to a person when shopping for apparel, you could have respondents go shopping with their cell phones and take pictures of the various clothes they're considering. They could send you texts about each item and why they do or don't want to purchase each one. You could also have them take a picture of the final item of clothing they purchased and answer a short survey via their cell phone after the shopping trip. This methodology allows one to gauge reactions to products in real time and to understand what is being considered, what is being rejected, what is finally purchased, and why. This method is particularly helpful for products that are bought without assistance and where memories of what was considered could be forgotten within a few days. Almost anything that is sold at a retail store is a candidate for this type of research—from small, inexpensive items (e.g., chewing gum, candy, soda) to larger items such as mattresses, clothing, shoes, or cars.

Another method we like involves prompting respondents via text messages to engage in certain behaviors (e.g., take medication) and then provide feedback (e.g., report how they are feeling). We can also prompt people at different times of the day to tell us what they're doing and what they're thinking and feeling at that time. This method can be instructive particularly for understanding what daily life is like for people who have certain challenges or for products/services one uses a lot and doesn't tend to think about. Another method that we like is to ask for internet video diaries, where respondents record their thoughts and feelings via webcam or cell phone over the course of several days/weeks for researchers to analyze.

Quantitative Research Methods

In this section, I discuss some of the major quantitative methods and their principal advantages and disadvantages. This section could be an entire book itself. Quantitative research can be complicated when one takes into account sampling, weighting of respondent data, and analysis of the results. These topics are beyond the scope of this book.

It's important to stress that when selecting a quantitative method, the final sample of respondents must represent a specific population. If the data doesn't represent that group accurately, it's worthless. Thus, the sampling frame is an extremely important part of evaluating each method. You want to think about who should participate in this type of quantitative research and why. In addition, we use a technique called click-balancing to census, which means that we monitor that all the potential respondent who click on the survey so they accurately represent the US population. Thus, we can be assured that a representative sample of people accessed the questionnaire.

Internet Surveys

Internet surveys have become the standard because so many people are online, and they're used to answering questions over the internet. In addition, the online population is fairly representative of the total population, particularly in North America. Internet surveys are the primary method we use. The major advantage of this method is that it allows researchers the opportunity to explore specific issues in detail by asking the right questions to specific people. If respondents say that they have a Toshiba computer, we can ask specific questions that relate only to Toshiba. Those who purchased their computer online would be asked a series of questions about how they decided to purchase it and what the advantages and disadvantages of buying online are for them.

Another advantage of doing internet surveys is that one can survey low-incidence populations—groups of consumers that are only one to five percent of the population. As a result, internet surveys are more affordable and less time-consuming than methods such as telephone surveys. If we have to make one hundred telephone calls to find one person who would qualify to answer our survey, we would be dialing thousands of numbers before we could obtain a sample size that would be useful for our analyses.

The major disadvantage of this method is that some consumer groups are difficult to reach with online surveys. The elderly and consumers with very low incomes are notable examples of people who may not be online as much as other groups. If they're online, they may not be as comfortable taking a survey over a computer. Because these groups are small but important, it's essential when designing a study to be aware that one may be excluding a group whose opinions should be heard.

Another potential disadvantage is the existence of "cheaters" or professional survey respondents who pose as particular types of people in order to do surveys for money. We have ways of weeding those people out of our work, but they can seriously undermine the eventual dataset of a study if there are large numbers of them. The other major problem that occurs are bots, which are computer programs that are created to take survey after survey in order to make money. These bots have become an increasing threat in today's market research and we've managed to find ways to reduce their threat in our work through careful questioning designed to trip them up. But it's a growing concern.

In-Person Surveys

The major advantage of using in-person surveys is that they catch people right after they've engaged in a behavior (e.g., purchased clothing), tried a product (e.g., drank a beverage), or had an experience (e.g., attended a seminar). Using traditional quantitative methods such as internet surveys allows time for memories to fade, which could lead to a biased recollection of the event and respondents' thoughts and feelings at the time. If you intercept people right after they've had an experience, you'll be more likely to get the most accurate perception.

We have surveyed people in a variety of situations in order to understand their perceptions of stores, events, and particular products or services. One of my favorite studies was for a consumer-goods company that wanted to understand if a shopping software program helped shoppers when purchasing mattresses. The company created the app that was accessed on a personal computer in the middle of the store. Several of these prototypes were created and placed in numerous stores. We then intercepted customers after they were done shopping and asked if had used the app and what they thought about it. We were able to discern how many customers actually approached computer with the app, how likely they were to use it again, and if the app gave them good or poor shopping recommendations. These research results told the company that the current program wasn't useful to customers and that it didn't provide good recommendations. As a result, the company decided to walk away from its invention and saved millions of dollars.

We have also recruited people to facilities where they try products and then answer a survey about their perceptions of and their likelihood to purchase these products. We regularly use this method to test our clients' products against competitors, and the results have been very predictive of how well these products perform in the marketplace. We've also done shelf-tests in facility where respondents react to a grocery shelf of actual and potential products. This type of research is very effective for understanding how people respond to actual retail shelf sets.

One disadvantage of this method is that respondents generally can only give a few minutes of their time. The average interview in an intercept survey is about three to five minutes—ten minutes is long—so the survey has to be thoughtfully crafted to make every second count. However, if you recruit individuals to a facility and have them try products, you can have a longer interview. Facility situations are somewhat less realistic but can be very useful for getting unbiased feedback about products and services.

Telephone Surveys

Telephone surveys were once as popular as internet surveys are today. One advantage of this method is that almost everyone has a phone, whereas some don't have internet access. In addition, a live interviewer can determine if the respondent understands the question and can repeat it if necessary. A respondent can also ask questions and get clarification if a question is unclear. Furthermore, an interviewer might be able to dissuade a respondent from hanging up if he gets bored by the questions. She might sense that her respondent is getting bored and say, "Just a couple more minutes." Another advantage of telephone surveys is that you can program skip patterns into them. Thus, if a respondent has a particular belief, follow-up questions can explore that belief in detail. The last advantage is that you know you're talking to a real person as opposed to a bot, which is a computer program that answers online surveys for money. This method also eliminates professional respondents who take surveys over and over via computer.

One of the major disadvantages of telephone surveys is that people filter out calls from people they don't know. Caller ID services allow people to see whether a family member or friend is calling. If a caller is not someone they know, people may be less likely to answer the telephone.

Another major disadvantage concerns cell phones. As of 2018, 90% of Americans currently have a cell phone and 77% have smart phones (Pew Research Center, 2018). However, less than half of households have a landline (Richter, 2018), which means that the majority of consumers live in cell phone only households. Federal law prohibits the use of automated dialers when calling cell phone numbers. As a result, cell phone-only respondents are often excluded from many studies because it's more expensive and time-consuming to reach them. Cell phone-only respondents, however, are likely to be different than those with landlines. We currently conduct telephone studies and we determine which numbers are cell numbers and which ones are not. Those that are cell number are dialed by an actual person and those that are landlines we use automatic dialers. For this study, we can't afford to have any bias in the final sample, so it's worth it.

Mail Surveys

Mail surveys provide an opportunity to contact people who aren't easily reached through the internet or by telephone. We used this method for a study we conducted with a group of residents of California who had immigrated to the United States and who spoke little or no English. Conducting a telephone survey would have been prohibitively expensive, given all the different languages we were targeting. We decided to conduct a mail survey that was translated into twelve different languages. This approach was a successful way of reaching each of the groups that we were interested in surveying.

The major disadvantage of mail surveys is that it's difficult to have the level of question specificity that you can have with telephone or internet surveys. You can't program skip patterns into mail surveys, and respondents don't easily follow instructions to skip in and out of questions. It's not always easy for respondents to follow logic such as "Skip to Q.23 and answer Section A." Mail surveys can also be expensive when you consider the cost of postage, particularly if the surveys are mailed to a large sample of people. Furthermore, this method has notoriously low response rates. I haven't conducted a mail survey in many years due to these disadvantages

Mixed Methods

One way to overcome the disadvantages of any method is to use a mixed-method design. You can combine two or even three different methods. For example, in a recent piece of work, we wanted to survey low-income consumers who shop at discount stores. We learned that many of these customers lived in rural areas, and some didn't have internet access. However, conducting mail or in-person intercept surveys with this group would have been very expensive. We suggested a mixed design that involved surveying customers who were online and then augmenting this data with surveys of customers who had been shopping in the stores and who weren't online. Thus, we had the advantages of the internet survey and its ability to drill into specific issues across a wide range of people. And we had the advantages of an in-person survey to talk with people who had just been shopping, so we could get their immediate reactions to the stores. This method allowed us to talk to shoppers who were online and those who were not.

Below is a table that summarizes some of the positive and negative aspects of each method.

Method	Strengths	Weaknesses
Telephone-depth interviews	Convenient for respondent. Can get into real depth with each person	Cannot see person's body language. Time consuming
In-person interviews	Depending on location, can be convenient for respondent Allow one to see person's body language Allow one to see context (e.g., work, office, home environment)	Time-consuming to conduct Time-consuming due to travel time to person's location Can be inconvenient for respondent if in facility Can be expensive if in facility
Observation research	Can see respondents using product or service and understand reasons for satisfaction/ dissatisfaction Can see work/ office/	Not worthwhile if respondents can readily tell you what they like/dislike Requires keen ability to observe; may miss much

	home environment and role that product/services play there	
Focus groups	Can talk to a large number of people in short period of time Can observe body language Group process can assist in understanding or solving an issue	Expensive Group dynamics can be problematic Dominant personalities can influence the group Groupthink and group polarization can skew results
Online discussion forums	Can be very convenient for respondents to do out of their homes or offices Allow people to process questions over the course of 3-5 days	Cannot see people or read body language People can "pose" as individuals who they are not
Online focus groups	Can be very convenient for respondents to do out of their home or office	Limited ability to see people and cannot read body language. People can "pose" as individuals who they are not
Mobile qualitative	Can understand immediate reactions to products/service, environments	Limited to only a few questions
In-person quantitative	Can obtain quantitative data and reactions to products/services that are not retrospective	May require an interviewer to administer. Some products may be difficult to test in person
Online quantitative	Very convenient for respondents to complete at the time and place that is most convenient.	If recalling things from the past, are reliant on memories.

Table 4: Strengths and Weaknesses of Different Research Methods

Designing the Study

Once you've decided on the type of method you want to use, it's time to design the study and specify how many focus groups or shop-alongs or surveys you want to conduct. We use several rules at Beall Research to help us design each study. These are general guidelines that we provide to clients.

Current Customers First

We generally design each research study with the assumption that the most important person is your current customer. Our belief is that you are most likely to sell more of your current product or service to current customers than anyone else. And you're also more likely to sell *a new product/service* to existing customers than you are to other groups. And if your advertising is to work, it certainly cannot alienate your current customers.

Generally, growth for a company occurs first with current customers and then extends to past and then potential customers. Imagine that you own a pet-supply store. You want to see if you could add pet-sitting services to your potential portfolio of services. The first group you would want to survey would be current customers. They're already coming into your store, they already buy your other products/services, and they obviously have a pet at home. You need to spend the lowest marketing dollars possible in order to get them to buy your new service. Past customers will be more expensive to acquire. These people may not use your products/services because they have found a competitor that they like better or because your location is no longer convenient for them. Finding and converting them back to customers will be more difficult than selling to current customers. Potential customers are those people who currently have a pet at home but who don't use your services/products. In order to get to this group of customers, you will have to find them, educate them about your offering, and then encourage them to buy a service from a store they don't know well. The lowest priority comprises non-customers, which is the group that doesn't buy the specific product/service and never plans to do so. They don't have pets or would never use a pet-sitting service.

Below is an overview of the hierarchy of customers for many marketing initiatives and market-research studies.

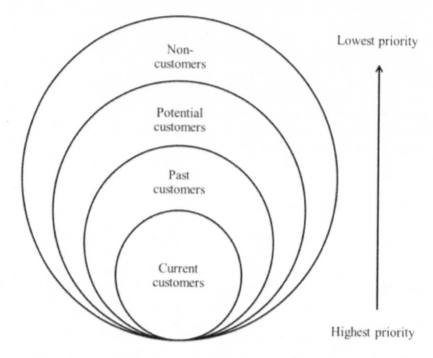

Figure 3: Hierarchy for Project Designs

So current customers are the most important targets, followed by past customers and potential customers. But you also want to think about what other variables could be important in your study. Is geography important? Would people in certain areas be more likely to buy this product or service? Would people who have a higher income be more interested? At this point, it's especially helpful to have a set of strong hypotheses to drive the design of the study.

For example, we conducted a research project for a major provider of lab equipment to hospitals. The client wanted to know why they were able to sell their equipment to some hospitals and not to others. They hypothesized that they're better able to sell this equipment to smaller hospitals because their product is ideally suited for low-volume labs. This client had done little research on this topic and the respondents are lab directors who are spread all over the country. We suggested conducting telephone-depth interviews, given their geographic dispersion and the fact that busy lab directors would prefer to talk via phone from their place of work. We suggested the following sample design.

Type of Laboratory	Won Account	Lost Account
Small Lab	8–10 Telephone-depth interviews (TDIs)	8–10 TDIs
Large Lab	8–10 TDIs	8–10 TDIs
TOTAL	**16–20 TDIs**	**16–20 TDIs**

Table 5: Research Design for Win–Loss Study

The Magic Numbers of 2, 5, and 10 for Qualitative Research

When we design our studies, we often use certain rules that have worked for us in the past. When it comes to focus groups, we tend to use the "rule of two"—we need to conduct two focus groups in any given geography or for any given group. If you conduct at least two focus groups and hear something unique in more than one group, you know you've heard something useful. But if you only conduct one group in California and the group tells you that they care deeply about water issues, you don't know if that opinion is representative of California or if that opinion represents people who tend to live in that area. If you hear the same opinion in two focus groups, you know it wasn't the one environmentalist who was part of the first focus group and that it could be a prevalent attitude. Generally, we recommend any project that uses focus groups to have at least three to nine focus groups.

Recently, we did a study for a major tire manufacturer who wanted to test some new advertising. They wanted to be sure that their advertising was equally appealing to different consumer segments as well as people in different parts of the country. We designed a study that sampled different age groups as well as different geographic regions. See the design below.

Age	Northeast	South	Midwest
Aged 18–24	1 focus group	1 focus group	1 focus group
Aged 25–39	1 focus group	1 focus group	1 focus group
Aged 40–59	1 focus group	1 focus group	1 focus group
TOTAL	3 focus groups	3 focus groups	3 focus groups

Table 6: Research Design for Age by Geography

With this design, we had three focus groups for each age group and three for each region of the country. Thus, if we heard everyone in one focus group aged eighteen to twenty-four saying something, we would have to hear it in the other two groups in that same age range in order to draw any major conclusions. And if we heard a particular concern or reaction in one group in the Northeast, we would have to hear that reaction in the other two groups in that region to identify whether there was a geographic difference.

When it comes to qualitative research done with individuals rather than groups, such as telephone-depth interviews, in-person interviews, or shop-alongs, we tend to rely on five to ten interviews with any given group. We believe hearing a particular attitude or observing a particular behavior across five to ten people is a significant finding. Thus, we tend to make sure we have multiple individuals for each cell of a research design. For example, in a study for a food manufacturer, we interviewed people who had children of different age groups in different parts of the country. The design is shown below.

Age of Children	Urban Area	Suburban Area	Rural Area
Mothers with children under age 5	5 in-home interviews	5 in-home interviews	5 in-home interviews
Mothers with children aged 6–12	5 in-home interviews	5 in-home interviews	5 in-home interviews
Mothers with children aged 13+	5 in-home interviews	5 in-home interviews	5 in-home interviews
TOTAL	15 in-home interviews	15 in-home interviews	15 in-home interviews

Table 7: Research Design for Age of Children by Area

The Magic Numbers of 100, 250, 500, and 1,000 for Quantitative Research

With quantitative research, we're looking to collect enough data to have a degree of confidence in the result and to be able to make any comparisons that we need to test current hypotheses. The magic numbers for this type of work vary between 100 and 1,000. We aim to have at least 100 respondents for any given cell of the research. The reason we tend to use 100 is because it has a confidence interval of ±10%.

It would be impossible to survey entire populations, so we do the next best thing: ask enough people that we're statistically certain to have the right answer. The statistic that tells us this information is called a confidence interval, which is an indicator that measures how much we can expect a given estimate to vary. If we learn that 50% of people in our sample said they love a product and we have a confidence interval of 10%, we know that the actual answer is likely to be 40–60% in the actual population. If we had a sample of 500 (and thus a confidence interval of $\pm 4\%$), we know that the actual answer is likely to be 46–54%.

We typically use a confidence level of 95%, which means that with repeated samples, we would expect that our estimates will fall within the confidence interval 95% of the time. Thus, if we repeated our study 100 times, we would expect that our result would fall into that specific interval 95 times out of 100. In our example above, we would expect that the percentage of people who love that product would be 46–54% for 95 of those 100 studies. See the table below, which shows some of the common sample sizes we use and their associated confidence intervals at the 95% level.

Sample Size	Confidence Interval for 95% Level
75	$\pm 11\%$
100	$\pm 10\%$
150	$\pm 8\%$
200	$\pm 7\%$
250	$\pm 6\%$
500	$\pm 4\%$
750	$\pm 4\%$
1,000	$\pm 3\%$
2,000	$\pm 2\%$

Table 8: Confidence Intervals for Common Sample Sizes

It's because of these confidence intervals that we tend to use the numbers 100, 250, 500, and 1,000 a great deal in our sample designs. Typically, we like to have 100–250 individuals in each sample cell with totals of 300–500 across groups and a final total of 1,000 or more. For example, we have a client who wants to understand charitable giving in different age groups in the United States. They also wanted to understand if people in different parts of the United States vary in giving. Below is the design we recommended.

Generation	Northeast	Midwest	South	West	TOTAL
Gen Z	125 Surveys	125 Surveys	125 Surveys	125 Surveys	500 Surveys
Millennials	125 surveys	125 surveys	125 surveys	125 surveys	500 surveys
Gen X	125 surveys	125 surveys	125 surveys	125 surveys	500 surveys
Baby Boomers	125 surveys	125 surveys	125 surveys	125 surveys	500 surveys
TOTAL	500 surveys	500 surveys	500 surveys	500 surveys	2,000 surveys

Table 9: Research Design for Generation by Area of the United States

With this design, we have enough of a sample to compare the generational groups against one another and to compare the geographic regions. We also have enough of a sample to provide some data about each generation within each geographic area.

For our clients who are making major decisions about whether to acquire or invest in a company, our sample sizes are much larger because they want a greater degree of precision and confidence around the answer. And for segmentation studies, where we will be subdividing and profiling the groups within a market, we use very large samples. In a recent study we did for a client that wanted to determine if they should acquire a major company, the sample looked something like the design below.

Type of Customer	Aged 18–30	Aged 31–50	Aged 51+	TOTAL
Current Customers of Company	500 surveys	500 surveys	500 surveys	1,500 surveys
Past Customers of Company	500 surveys	500 surveys	500 surveys	1,500 surveys
Potential Customers Who Would Consider Buying from Company	500 surveys	500 surveys	500 surveys	1,500 surveys
TOTAL	1,500 surveys	1,500 surveys	1,500 surveys	4,500 surveys

Table 10: Research Design for Type of Customers

CHAPTER 5:
INVESTIGATING
CONSUMER EMOTIONS
IN QUALITATIVE AND
QUANTITATIVE
RESEARCH

O e of the major lessons that I've learned in analyzing consumer behavior is that emotions propel a lot of human beings' actions. The reason feelings motivate so much of our behavior is because they're hardwired into us as a species. Our emotions are the reason that we're here today. Our ancestors didn't think a whole lot when they first saw a woolly mammoth. They didn't cogitate about how fast it runs, whether it seems angry, whether it eats meat or whether it would eat them...they just felt fear and started to run.

As you begin to design your study, emotions are an important aspect to consider because they're so strongly linked to behavior. Emotions are so integral to our actions that we often feel compelled to behave in certain ways when we experience them. When we're sad we withdraw, when happy we engage, when angry we fight. When we're surprised, we open our eyes wider to evaluate our surroundings. As a result, understanding emotions toward brands, products and services will lead us to understand the behavior of buyers toward these things.

Another reason we want to understand emotions is because they're linked to memory. Think about your life in retrospect and you'll remember the highs and the lows. You won't remember the regular days. The reason for that is probably due to a desire to increase positive emotional experiences and decrease negative ones. And given that emotions are related to our ancestor's survival, focusing on ways to manage these emotions make sense. We want to have fewer frightening experiences and more happy ones. Thus, humans are strongly motivated to engage in positive emotional experiences—whether that's through interactions with people or through products and services.

Emotions Guide Decision Making

It's a common belief in Western culture that good decisions occur when we subtract our emotions from the decision process and rely solely on reason. In actuality, the reverse is true. We tend to make better decisions when our emotions are involved, and we make worse decisions when they're not. Some of the most fascinating research in this area has been done with people who have normal cognitive functioning but cannot process emotional signals because of brain lesions. These people are the epitome of rational decision-makers because they don't process any emotional information when deciding what to do. Contrary to popular thought, researchers have found that these unemotional decision-makers actually make poor decisions or no decisions (Bechara 2004). They just aren't motivated by their emotions, so they have been known to bankrupt themselves because they don't feel fear or they make no decisions because they just don't feel the need.

Because emotions are related to decision making, humans use them as a gut check on whether to engage or not with brands, products, services and people. The emotional system that consumers use is a valence-intensity system where consumers are drawn to engage with things that give them a positive emotional response and pushed away from things that generate a negative one. Human beings often have an emotional response to all things—and that response varies from positive to neutral to negative. And they experience that response at higher or lower intensities. Thus, one may have an intensely positive or negative response to a new product on the shelf. If the reaction is a highly positive one, that generally leads to engagement. If the reaction is a strongly negative one, that leads to avoidance. And often consumers don't even know why they have they have the reaction that they do, but they follow the lead of their emotions. These reactions are a type of automatic "thinking" that is called Type 1 (Kahneman, 2013) and it probably occurs the majority of the time You can likely see this in your own behavior. You see a new product on a shelf or watch a digital ad on your computer. You immediately have a response to it: positive, negative or neutral. The intensity of that response will determine the level at which you engage with what you see. If you have a negative reaction to something, you'll move along. And if you have a positive reaction, you'll move in a bit closer to explore it. See the figure below for a visual depiction of the emotional system.

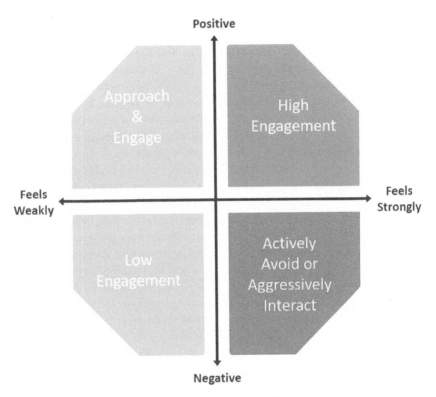

Figure 4: Intensity-Valence System for Emotions

In much of the work we do, we often see that immediate emotional reaction that respondents have to a variety of things we're testing. In a recent study for a laundry product, we videotaped all respondents' first facial reactions to a new scented laundry product that they would be taking home to use for a month. Although many of the women who were testing the product gave high ratings to it, their facial reactions showed us that their emotional responses were not always positive. At the end of the study, we were able to show that those who had an initial negative emotional response to the product didn't end up using it after the study concluded—even after using it for an entire month!

Measuring Immediate Emotional Reactions

Because people use their emotions as guides, the products, services, people and brands we approach and engage with are the ones that we generally have a positive emotional response to in the world. As a result, it's important to understand the immediate emotional reaction that people have to brands, packaging, advertising and products/services in concept form. We measure these reactions both qualitative and quantitatively. In qualitative research where we videotape respondents or they upload videos of themselves, we code their facial expressions to identify emotional responses. We use our own coding system and don't rely on facial-analysis software because we haven't found any that is as accurate as our trained coders—who are often able to see subtle and nuanced expressions.

We also have coded facial expressions and nonverbal behavior real-time in shopper situations. In one study that we conducted for a pet-food manufacturer, we had consumers participate in a shopping study where they shopped in a major mass-market retailer. We set up a test shelf that had new pet-food products on it and we also had a traditional shelf that had the pet-food products they normally carry. We had consumers shop both aisles and we coded their facial reactions and body language as they shopped each one. We then asked them to provide ratings for each aisle, identify what they liked and disliked about each one, and then explain if they preferred one aisle over the other and why. Although consumers claimed they preferred one aisle more than the other, they were unable to identify what the differences were and often described spurious reasons for their preference. However, when we analyzed the facial and nonverbal reactions, we could see that the new aisle was more engaging and engendered expressions and articulations of surprise and delight. Consumers also purchased more in the new aisle. The results of this work were used to identify clear changes that could be made in the pet-food aisle that would positively impact the retailer and the manufacturer.

Another way that we measure emotional reactions is through self-reported ratings that occur immediately after respondents have been exposed to a brand, product, service, communication, etc. People are sometimes surprised that we measure emotions via self-reported ratings, but we've found that if you ask questions immediately after (and sometimes we put a time-limit on how long they see the question), we get a clear indication of how positively or negatively their response is to the stimulus. We do have a variety of ways to get at these self-reported feelings so we measure their response using several different types of questions, which can vary based on the category we're researching. We've found that these immediate reactions either through facial and nonverbal behavior or through self-report are invaluable.

Emotional Identification with Brands, Products, Services & Communications

Another area that's very useful for understanding human behavior is the extent to which consumers emotionally identify with something in the marketplace. We've found that the level to which consumers see a brand's offering as something that's for people like them and that represents something important to them, the more likely they are to buy it. Consumers have many choices about what to purchase and they're drawn to those things that affirm who they are and that make them feel good about themselves.

I had this experience recently at a Walgreen's store. I was shopping in the cosmetic aisle and saw a new brand that I'd not seen before. I was immediately drawn to it because it was colorful and very feminine. That was my immediate emotional response to it. I moved in closer for an inspection and suddenly had the feeling that these were products for teenagers. I didn't spend much time after that, but my sudden assessment that these were not products designed for women of my age group pushed me away and sent me toward other brands.

Brands that speak to us with products and services that seem designed for people like us and that remind us of our values and the people and experiences that are important to us are going to win in the marketplace. Brands that get tied up in talking about their products in terms of features and attributes are less likely to be successful. Coca-Cola is a great example of a brand that could talk about the attributes of its main beverage, but instead focuses on the important moments in your life when you drink their beverage. They have a strong association with Christmas. In fact, their advertisement, *Taste the Feeling*, clearly shows how the product will make you feel and the important times in your life when it will be present. It shows people having snowball fights with friends, lovers kissing, making food, going to concerts and playing music. And it ends with smiling happy people and says: Taste the Feeling. It's brilliant.

Feelings About Self

The last area of emotional inquiry that we've found to be extremely useful is how people feel about themselves as a result of owning and using specific brands. We recently conducted a study where we looked at how 17 major brands made people feel about themselves when they owned and used them. Different brands made people feel different things about themselves. Some brand made people feel attractive, others people feel stylish. The brands that made people feel the best about themselves were purchased more frequently, more likely to be recommended and the ones consumers were willing to pay more to own. For example, below is a word cloud that summarizes how owners of the brand Apple feel about themselves when owning and using Apple's products. As you can see, people felt confident, intelligent and proud of themselves as a result of buying this brand. I'm not sure about you, dear reader, but any product or service that makes me feel more confident and intelligent is going to be high on my list to purchase.

Figure 5: Feelings About Self When Using Apple Brand

Feelings when Using

Another major area of that influences the likelihood to purchase again are the feelings that people have when they use certain brands products/services. In the study our firm conducted, we found that there is an emotional journey that customers go on when they buy things. Although that journey is different for distinct brands, there are some commonalities that occur. In general, we found that it's not the absence of a negative feelings when using something that predicts repeat purchasing, it's the presence of a positive one. Interestingly, if consumers have a single very negative experience, as long as they have another equally positive one, their likelihood to purchase that product/service again is high.

We've used the concept of the *emotional journey* very effectively to help our clients understand where customers convert and buy, where they become loyal advocates, and where they become disillusioned and abandon a brand. Emotions are powerful because they're linked to memory and are more likely to be recalled. We will remember the rude customer-service person or the first time we used something and how it didn't work, or how we received admiration from someone when they saw our new handbag. These are the moments that stick with us and they're what we tell family and friends. They're also the memories we call to mind when thinking about buying something again.

Qualitative Techniques for Identifying Feelings

So how do good researchers unearth the messy, sticky emotional world of individuals they interact with for only a short period of time? We do it carefully. Respondents don't typically want to have a therapy session and delve into their inner emotional lives while participating in a research study. They don't want to resolve inner conflicts or understand how childhood experiences have marred them. However, we need to know the role that emotions play in a particular set of perceptions and behaviors. Getting to the heart of respondents' emotions involves using tools and techniques that allow participants to express their feelings in a way that makes them feel safe and that provides us with useful information. Some of the ways we obtain the emotional piece of a decision include the following:

- Asking directly

- Projective techniques
- Associations
- Accessing hopes, dreams, and aspirations
- Storytelling
- Salient memories

Asking Directly

Believe it or not, sometimes just asking the questions about how people feel can be enough to generate the information about their emotional response to brands. As long as people feel comfortable and accepted for expressing themselves, they will provide great insight into how they feel. Years ago, I conducted focus groups with men who had stage four prostate cancer. The client was unsure if a woman could get the men to express how they felt about such an intimate issue. There was no need for concern because the men told me incredibly intimate details about themselves and their fears about impotence and dying. Several men cried openly in the group. It's one of the most emotional focus groups I ever moderated.

Creating an atmosphere where emotional expression is acceptable and even encouraged is a key component to having respondents express themselves. Good moderators begin their sessions by encouraging people to be honest and to openly express their thoughts and feelings. They also use their nonverbal expressions to create a comfortable, accepting environment. When respondents express themselves openly and honestly, the moderator can respond nonverbally in ways that say that such sharing is acceptable, such as giving good eye contact and nodding when someone shares. As a result, people will begin to be expressive in response to one another, which can encourage more sharing of inner feelings. It's not unusual in some of my focus groups for the respondents to begin sharing things that are deeply personal and highly emotional, such as fears about a loved one dying, and then to have others expound on these emotional experiences in great depth. I've seen more than my share of tears from respondents who have felt comfortable enough to express their deepest feelings in a group discussion.

And having people indicate their feelings on paper before discussing them can be useful. In focus groups we regularly have respondents indicate their feelings about an advertisement and how intensely they felt it. Because they put the feelings on paper, they become comfortable with their experience and when everyone describes their emotional responses, it

Projective Techniques

Another way to elicit respondents' emotions is to use projective techniques that allow people to share their feelings in a nonthreatening way. One common projective technique we use is to ask respondents to imagine that someone else is experiencing something and to ask them to imagine how that other person feels. For example, we might be interested in all the fears that people have when buying a car, so we would ask them to describe feelings that other people have when they buy a car. We can specifically ask them to discuss any fears that people have during this process. This technique allows people to discuss their feelings without personalizing them. Projective exercises like this one are particularly useful with people who are uncomfortable describing some of their feelings because they don't want to appear vulnerable.

Another projective technique that we use involves characters. We use characters that represent thoughts and feelings and have respondents identify the character that is most like them. In one study we did with physicians, we put pictures of different characters up on the walls. Some of these characters were superheroes like Captain America, and some of them were Peanuts characters. In one picture, Snoopy was hanging on to a trapeze, but just barely. We asked the physicians to describe which character represented them, and several identified the scared Snoopy as the character that represented their reaction to treating certain diseases. The characters allowed them to express certain emotions in a way that was not threatening to them. However, in more formal focus-group discussions, physicians tend not to divulge their feelings of fear and worry. We also use celebrities as a way to allow people to project their feelings onto others. Some celebrities, depending on the current tabloid news, can represent a variety of thoughts and feelings for people.

Associations

We also use the technique of associations to elicit emotional content. Sometimes we give the name of a brand and have people tell us the words they associate with it. Let's imagine that we're researching a brand of fictional toothpaste called "Natural Toothpaste." We would say the brand name, and then respondents would say the words they associate with this brand. After doing numerous interviews or focus groups, we might learn that specific words are strongly associated with this brand. For example, we might have learned that *snobby, expensive, rich,* and *arrogant* are the words most associated with this brand.

Another effective technique for ascertaining some of the gut-level associations people have is to understand the imagery associated with a product or service. One way to do this is by having respondents create collages. We have stacks of popular magazines that we provide to respondents, and we ask them to cut out any image that reminds them of a brand. This technique is associative, so respondents tend to pull images that capture a thought or feeling they have about a product. Images convey a richer set of feelings than just words. For example, a pharmaceutical company wanted to understand how a particular new medication is perceived by looking at all imagistic associations people have with it. We learned that people associate very specific colors and images with this medication. The result of this work was used to create the look and feel of this new brand. To see a fictional example of a beverage brand with certain imagery, see the next picture. As you can see in this hypothetical example, this brand has strong associations with movement, speed, physical activity, the outdoors, and sports.

Figure 6: Imagery Associated with Hypothetical New Beverage

Laddering

Once you understand the associations that people have to a product, service or brand, you can do a laddering exercise, which ultimately creates output like that shown in the figure below. The output shows you what the higher order associations and ultimately higher-order benefits are for a specific brand or product/service. In the hypothetical beverage example, one might find that the first set of associations are with speed, physical activity and the outdoors. When we then ask about associations with this set of things, we might learn that speed is associated with race cars, physical activities is associated with health and the outdoors is associated with being rugged and natural. If we then go on to understand the associations with race cars, health and the outdoors, we may learn that the major association is masculinity and confidence. Thus, the higher order benefit consumers might obtain to purchasing this beverage is feeling more masculine and confident because they have these higher-order associations to this product.

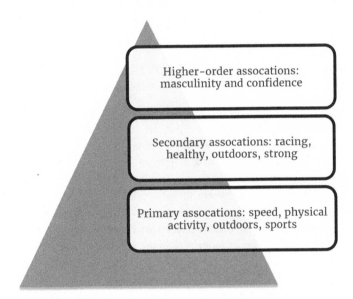

Figure 7: Simplified Example of Laddering Output

Hopes, Dreams, and Aspirations

A very useful technique that we use is to engage people's hopes, dreams, and aspirations. By understanding a person's hopes and dreams, we can understand some of the emotions that he has about the things that he buys. I believe that people don't buy stuff; they buy visions of the future and perceptions of who they want to be. When a man buys exercise equipment, what exactly is he buying? I would argue that, at some level, he is buying a desired vision of himself, and that he sees a future person who looks good and who accrues certain rewards as a result. Clearly, his hopes and dreams play a large role in his purchase decision. In numerous categories, we have discovered that people buy products and services to bolster a specific self-perception. We are always intrigued by people who are not wealthy, but who use everyday purchases like coffee to give themselves a feeling of luxury and show the world that they have money. In so many categories, a purchase is not just a statement about oneself but a ticket to a lifestyle that people want. By understanding these desires, we are touching their emotional experience for that purchase. When people buy a time-share, are they buying a vacation, or are they hoping for more quality time with loved ones and better relationships with family? When you understand the emotions associated with a purchase, you've come a long way to understanding the decision to buy.

Stories and Memories

Stories are another way to understand the emotions that people have about products and services. We have people tell us stories about how they decided to purchase something and how they experienced it. These stories may sound random at first, but when we start to look at stories across many people, we see common themes. When we talked with young couples about their furniture purchases, we learned that these couples were not just telling us about the furniture in their homes; they were often telling us the stories of their relationships. The purchase of furniture was often a symbolic behavior that meant commitment, permanency, and the blending of two styles into one. Thus, the emotions around furniture purchasing were very deep and quite central to the young couples in their quest for a new life together.

Memories are another way to understand the emotional part of decision making. We ask respondents to tell us salient memories they have of the times they have used products. We may ask them, "Tell us about the first time you heard of Pepsi," "What is your first memory of Pepsi?" "Which celebrities can you remember drinking Pepsi?" "Tell me about times with your friends when you were drinking Pepsi," and so on. All of these memories have an emotional valence to them, and they begin to sum up a person's experience of a brand. We look at these memories and analyze them because the emotional themes that run through these memories are similar across groups of people and reveal the emotional components of a brand.

Measuring Emotions Quantitatively

Measuring emotions quantitatively generally involves asking respondents to provide insight into how they feel about various things. We measure a variety of feelings and some of the ways that we quantify emotions involve the following measures:

- Which emotions are felt in response to certain brands, products/services, advertising, etc.
- How intensely emotions are felt
- What associations occur in response to brands, products/services
- What emotions occur with each association
- How intensely emotions are experienced to these associations
- How people feel about themselves as a result of owning/using
- How people expect to feel if owned/used what we're investigating
- How well the brand/product/service represents people, their values, the experiences and individuals who are important to them

We also use imagery and have respondents select images that represent associations, feelings and experiences related to whatever we're investigating. This technique can be useful especially when it's based off the qualitative findings. Once we've uncovered how and why people feel the way they do, we can use images to quantify these complex inner experiences.

The last way we measure emotions quantitatively is by coding the facial expressions and nonverbal behavior through videos or real-time when we're with the person. This coding is done quite surreptitiously by a note taker who is observing the interview. This technique is used in qualitative research.

CHAPTER 6: OBTAINING THE DEPTH REQUIRED FOR INSIGHT

O nce we identify the strategic questions, the major hypotheses, and the research design, the real work begins. It's not enough to assume that because we've done everything right up to this point, the answer will fall into our lap. Insight is the result of looking at something deeply and seeing it in a different way, which leads to that "aha." It's the level of depth that makes the difference. Over the years, I've noticed that there are several practices that can help in obtaining the depth required for real insight. If one is conducting qualitative research, there may be an opportunity to observe something no one has seen before or to ask a question in a way that yields a nugget of wisdom. There are also opportunities to manage a research project so that the process reveals a deeper understanding as the project continues.

Hearing beyond the Words

One thing that I've learned is that you have to interpret what people tell you to understand what they really mean. For example, some respondents don't want to tell you how they really feel about a product because they worry about hurting someone's feelings. Despite assurances that I have had nothing to do with the creation of a product, I distinctly get the feeling that some people are trying to be polite by not telling me that the product we're discussing is a real stinker. One of the things that respondents will say is that a service is great for someone other than themselves. When they say, "It would be great for my aunt or my mother, but not for me," I know that they would never purchase it. The other thing that people say is that they can't imagine using a certain product now, but they think they might use it in the future. The translation of that sentence is, "I don't like it or need it now, but I might change my mind." If they don't want it now, I have no reason to believe they will want it in the future.

We pay close attention to what people say about when they think they will purchase something. Respondents' estimates on timing often reveal the truth about their purchase intent. We did focus groups with wealthy consumers in which we tested a new type of luxury mattress. We first talked about the concept and then showed them the specific mattress. All the consumers loved it. We asked them if they would purchase this mattress, and most said they would. We then told them to imagine that the mattress is currently available and asked how soon they would purchase it. Most of them said they would purchase it in a couple of years. The fact that the respondents could not envision buying the mattress for a couple of years told us that they were not completely sold on it. When we probed them about the reason for their timing, many admitted that they had some doubts about this particular mattress.

Another thing that people sometimes say is to "make it cheaper" after they learn the price of a product. Consumers want to maximize their money, and they have a selfish interest in telling us to make products less expensive for them. However, something else is going on here. When respondents tell us that something should be less expensive, what they're really saying is that the product doesn't provide enough value for them. Unless the price is inflated, the issue is not the cost. Americans are willing to pay good money for all kinds of things. If something is perceived as providing a significant value to them and their loved ones, they will buy it. When people tell us to make something cheaper, they are generally telling us that whatever we're discussing is not something that provides enough benefits for them to buy it. If the issue really is price, we can discern this problem by asking what people would pay. On many occasions, we have seen that respondents will give a nominal figure in response, which tells us that a service has little value for them.

Sometimes it's not what people say, but what they do. We did a project for a personal-care company, and the client was interested in understanding how women select shampoo. We convened a focus group of women and asked them what was important for them when it came to shampoo. The women told us that a shampoo couldn't dry out their hair and that it had to leave their hair feeling soft and silky. They told us that a shampoo couldn't be too expensive, but if it made their hair look good, it was worth a few extra dollars. We then put out several bottles of shampoo on the table, and the women immediately opened the bottles and smelled the shampoo.

Interestingly, none of the women had mentioned fragrance as a major reason for buying shampoo, but it became obvious that fragrance was a major aspect of the purchase decision. Fragrance is probably the first thing women evaluate in a shampoo, followed by its performance. In so many different studies, it's the things that people don't say that speak volumes. I discuss nonverbal communication and how you can read the hidden communication of research respondents in the next chapter.

Asking the Same Question in Different Ways

Generally, qualitative research projects involve creating a discussion guide and then following the general flow of the guide in a somewhat conversational form. Often, the same question is asked of many different groups to determine if there is some consistency among people in their responses. However, one of the most useful techniques you can employ in qualitative research is to ask a question in numerous ways to understand the parameters of an answer. One example of this phenomenon occurred with shaving research. Typically, men complain about having to shave every day. However, one clever moderator asked how men would feel about a product that would effectively make shaving a memory. Suddenly, the men started to explain that shaving is an important masculine ritual and that losing that ritual would be undesirable. By asking about shaving in a variety of ways, the moderator learned the myriad thoughts and feelings men have about this subject.

There are many ways to ask the same question. The shaving example asks people to imagine their lives without something. Other techniques include asking respondents to imagine that they are the CEO of a specific brand and inquiring about what they would do differently. We've also asked people what a good advertisement would be for a new service. In some studies, we've asked people to design the perfect product or service experience based on their current needs. All of these approaches reveal important things about what respondents really think and feel about something.

Probing and Probing

Another way to gain depth in qualitative work is to spend a great deal of time probing respondents' answers to questions. We generally don't take the first response to a question as the final answer. It's usually more complicated than that. So when respondents tell us that they like something, we ask them what they specifically like about it, and then we ask which things they like most, and so on. We once had a client who told us that diabetic patients didn't mind having diabetes, and she sent me some focus-group tapes to prove her point. The moderator had a group of diabetic respondents, and she asked them what it was like to have diabetes. Many of them responded that it was occasionally problematic but something that they had gotten used to having. The moderator then went on to another question. As a result of her lack of probing, the client interpreted the first response as the final answer. If the moderator had probed about what was problematic about diabetes and what the respondents had specifically gotten used to, she would have understood the emotional response to this disease much better.

Managing a Qualitative Project to Achieve Depth

Another major way to achieve depth in qualitative research is to manage the project so that subsequent focus groups, interviews, or discussion forum sessions don't duplicate the previous ones. One of my mentors used to remind me that the word *focus* in *focus group* refers to getting a clearer, more focused understanding of the issues over time. He recommended having a different discussion during the last focus-group session than during the first one. He believed that the initial superficial conversations change over time and become more thoughtful. By the time the groups are finished, the initial learning has been explored to a much deeper level.

This technique is called the iterative approach, and we use it effectively for many different kinds of projects. We use this approach frequently with communications work. Our advertising-agency partners will observe focus groups through a two-way mirror and then revise concept statements, taglines, and advertising communications between the groups based on what we've learned in each session. The result is that we have materials that are very different (and much better) by the end of several focus groups.

The other technique we use is to inquire what questions client observers have between sessions. Usually, a set of questions will lead to more questions, and so on. This iterative-question approach engages the observers of the research and shows the moderators what they need to focus on and explore more deeply. In a recent project that we did for a discount store, the client said that she needed answers to particular questions. Once she had answers to these initial questions, new ones emerged. The answers to the new questions in turn begot more questions. This project is a good example of one for which the last focus group was completely different than the first one, and for which we had a more thorough understanding because we used this iterative approach.

Testing Potential Scenarios

One of my clients is a private-equity firm that invests in other companies. They sometimes determine if they want to make an investment based on quantitative market research about an industry and a specific company within it. One way they evaluate a potential acquisition is by measuring how customers of that company will respond to different scenarios. These scenarios could be actions that the future owners might take once they own the company, or they could be the actions of major competitors. In some cases, we've tested what would happen if a major competitor offered a similar product or service or undercut the target investment company on pricing. These scenarios give my client a unique view of whether the company they are thinking of acquiring provides something that's uniquely valuable in the marketplace and how problematic it would be if competitors took certain actions.

You can test potential scenarios in both quantitative and qualitative research. In quantitative work, you can present specific scenarios and then measure consumers' likelihood to purchase, switch to a competitor or cease buying the product/service. In qualitative work, you can test scenarios with questions such as "What if a competitor offered you a similar product?" or "What if this service became more expensive?" or "What if a competitor offered the same service for less money?" We also ask respondents to imagine brands offering new products and services: "What if Brand X now offered this potential product?" The qualitative and quantitative answers to these questions can yield valuable information about how loyal people are, how much people would be willing to pay for things, and how easily certain products can be replaced.

Another way to test scenarios quantitatively is with conjoint and discrete choice analysis. This type of analysis is just one major "what if?" question that is used to evaluate different product configurations. Respondents are offered several product configurations, such as: 1) I-phone X with 65 GB of storage, 3D touch screen and 4 GB of RAM for $1,000, or 2) Samsung Galaxy S10 phone with 128 GB of storage, unbreakable screen, and 6 GB of RAM for $999. In this case, the brand is different, the price is similar, but the memory and the screen are different. Respondents are given many different cell phone configurations and asked how likely they would be to purchase each one. These ratings allow us to determine how important different features are in specific products so we can simulate different offerings in the market and estimate demand for them. We have also done qualitative conjoint projects in the context of focus groups to understand the role that different features play in making a product or service more or less attractive.

Using Open-Ended Questions in Quantitative Research

The last way we can obtain depth in quantitative research is by offering respondents the option to write in their thoughts and feelings in an open-ended format. We often ask people to explain what they like or dislike about a product and whether it has performed according to their expectations. Respondents may write a sentence or a paragraph about their experiences or perceptions about something. These responses are then evaluated by experts who group these responses into "codes." Codes are the common responses that people give to each question. Each response is assigned to one or more codes, and we calculate the percentage of people who volunteered that reason or perception. Thus, we might find that one of the things people like about an online grocer is the ability to reject bad produce because 35 percent of people volunteered that response as a major reason they prefer this retailer.

Another way that we use open-ended responses is to allow respondents the chance to write in their own reason or perception if it's not represented in the response categories of a question. Survey designers often think they have exhausted all potential response categories when they write a question, but respondents may feel differently. Thus, we offer them the opportunity to write in their responses in an "other" category. These open-ended answers are then coded, and the percentage of people who gave each response is tabulated. Occasionally, you'll find that one response surfaces among a large percentage of respondents. Other times, you may find that very little useful data emerges, which lets you know that you captured the most important response categories in the survey. Although open-ended questions can sometimes be expensive, they are well worth it.

CHAPTER 7: READING THE HIDDEN COMMUNICATIONS OF RESEARCH RESPONDENTS IN QUALITATIVE RESEARCH

S ometimes it's what respondents *don't* say that can be the most revealing. In general, body language, or nonverbal communication, is a rich source of insight about what people think and feel about a topic. I like to say that you can choose not to speak, but you can never be silent nonverbally. I spend a great deal of time watching respondents' body language because they sometimes tell me more with their bodies than they do with their words. Regardless of whether you are a moderator or a person observing research respondents, being able to read body language can be very useful.

In this chapter, I discuss PERCEIVE™, which is the method of reading nonverbal communication that I developed many years ago. It is one way of "perceiving" other people that I have found useful because it sums up all the parts of the complex system of nonverbal behavior. It's also easy to remember. Each letter of PERCEIVE™ refers to a major piece of nonverbal communication. *P* stands for proximity; *E* is for expressions; *R* is for relative orientation; *C* is for contact (physical touching); *E* is for eyes; *I* is for individual gestures; *V* is for voice; and the last *E* stands for existence of adaptors, which are those small fidgety behaviors that people do when they're stressed or bored.

You may be wondering how PERCEIVE™ was developed and what the basis is for it. Why not OBSERVE or SEE or ASPARAGUS? PERCEIVE™ was born after an exhaustive review of hundreds of studies that were conducted by academic researchers. The research literature revealed some basic findings about nonverbal communication that have been replicated in numerous studies. PERCEIVE™ describes the major areas of nonverbal communication: the face, body, voice, and hands. As an aside, this research was mostly conducted in English-speaking societies such as the United States, Canada, and Australia, and the findings accurately summarize Western cultures. The basic principles of what we will discuss, however, apply to most societies.

Proximity

Proximity refers to the amount of distance people place between themselves and others. Generally, people tend to sit and stand near people they like and want to get to know. They tend to stand away from those whom they dislike or believe they have little in common with. I always find it interesting that people tend to sit and stand near those who are similar to them. I cannot tell you how many times all the women in a focus group have sat together and how often the men have done the same thing. This phenomenon also occurs with race. People of similar races tend to sit near one another. In a focus group we conducted in the Southern United States, all the African Americans sat on one side of the table, while all the Caucasians sat on the other side.

As a moderator, I watch whom people sit and stand near. I also watch the degree of proximity that they have to me as a moderator. Not surprisingly, when people are engaged and interested in a topic, they tend to sit forward in their chairs and to lean toward the moderator; their proximity *increases*. When they are disinterested and disengaged, their proximity *decreases*. I also watch how closely respondents sit and stand next to one another in observational research, in-home interviews, and shop-along research. The closer the relationship, the closer the proximity tends to be between two people.

Expressions

Expressions refer to facial expressions that people make regularly. Researchers who study facial expressions across cultures have found that there are six basic emotional expressions that all cultures recognize and have a word to describe. These basic expressions are happiness, sadness, anger, fear, surprise, and disgust (Ekman & Friesen 1975). Some theorists believe that contempt is a basic expression, but others disagree. I will include it in our discussion. These basic expressions may be hardwired into us as a species, and all other expressions use some form of these basic ones (Ekman & Friesen 1975). For example, you might have an expression that is partly surprise and partly happiness if you walk into your own surprise birthday party.

In general, people don't show exaggerated facial expressions. There are cultural display rules that dictate which emotional expressions are appropriate for specific situations. Thus, if your boss suggests that you stay late to work on a project, you probably wouldn't want to openly express anger to her. Although you're not thrilled, you will be professional and politely explain that you can stay for a couple of hours tonight and that you will come in early tomorrow to finish your work. Your expressions are in line with the cultural display rules for this situation. You didn't express anger—or did you?

Researchers have learned that when people feel something, they actually express something called a microexpression, which is an expression that lasts for about one-fifth of a second and is not typically seen by others (Ekman 2003). The reason this expression occurs is because we are hardwired to express certain emotions— particularly those basic ones just described. When we start to feel something internally, that feeling triggers muscles in our faces. We suppress a full expression before it occurs, and the result is a microexpression, which lasts for such a short period of time that a very small percentage of people will notice it. Have you ever seen a flash of an expression, but weren't sure if you saw something? You probably saw a microexpression.

Microexpressions are extremely useful in research situations because they reveal the immediate reactions that respondents have to products, services, brands, people, and specific parts of a discussion. The momentary expression yields valuable insight into what respondents are really feeling and thinking. As a moderator, when I see a microexpression, I don't call attention to it, but I allow the respondent to tell me another point of view. For example, in an in-home interview that we conducted with couples about financial services, a wife had a microexpression of contempt in response to some of the financial services her husband had purchased. After I saw the expression, I said that some people like these services and others don't. I asked her to tell me some of the reasons that people don't like these services. She could then tell me why she didn't like the financial services her husband bought without embarrassing him.

Seeing and reacting to microexpressions is not something that comes naturally to most people. One of the pioneers in this area is Paul Ekman. He created a CD-ROM that you can purchase to train yourself how to spot these expressions. After I trained myself to spot them, I was amazed at how often they occur. If the CD is not available, I encourage you to watch interviews in which the interviewer asks some controversial questions. If you slow down the recording, you can often see microexpressions on the faces of the people being interviewed.

Relative Orientation

Relative orientation refers to the degree of orientation that people have toward others. In general, the more interested we are in people, the more directly we orient ourselves toward them. Look at the next picture on the left. The couple in this picture is oriented almost directly toward one another. One of the first signs that an interaction between two people is beginning is that they start to orient their bodies toward one another. One of the first signs that an interaction is ending is when one or both people start to turn their bodies away. See the next picture on the right for an example. In this photo, the woman pictured on the right has started to turn her body away. Often, you can tell who is interested in whom by a person's orientation. In a few focus groups, we've had a respondent who wanted to be a moderator herself. She looked at the focus-group experience as a way to dominate a discussion. We can generally spot this situation within the first ten minutes of the group by her orientation. If she wanted to moderate the group, she would tend to orient herself toward the rest of the group members and away from the moderator. We have a way of handling this situation that is very effective. We use our orientation and other nonverbal cues to establish my authority.

Orientation can tell us how engaged people are with others. In the situation described above, some of the respondents did not like the respondent's attempt to moderate the focus group, and they oriented themselves away from her and toward me. I always notice orientations when doing in-home interviews. Sometimes a couple is more oriented toward each another than they are toward the interviewer. Sometimes that's the way I like it. Sometimes in focus groups, the respondents are more focused on one another than on the moderator. It becomes a true group discussion that does not need a facilitator, and the orientations of the respondents show that fact. I like that also.

Direct Orientation

Ending a Conversation

Contact

Contact refers to physical contact between two people. Physical contact is somewhat scripted among strangers and typically occurs with a handshake when people say hello or good-bye. However, outside of this scripted handshake, physical touch indicates liking, comfort, and familiarity with another person. Thus, we tend to touch those we like, those we are most familiar with, and those we are comfortable enough to touch.

Because touching is scripted among strangers, respondents generally don't touch me during interviews. However, respondents will occasionally shake my hand if they have been affected by their participation in a research project. Respondents will also touch one another if they have a close relationship or if they have been affected by another person. In some of my sessions, respondents become very emotional about an experience they are having. In a project with people who have a pulmonary disease, the respondents started to talk about how they cope with their situation. A young woman was not dealing well with her health, and the woman next to her encouraged her with several slight touches on the shoulder. Her touch of the other woman was an effort to comfort her, but it also revealed that she liked the young woman enough to touch her.

Respondents who know one another well sometimes touch each other, and their physical contact, or lack thereof, can say a lot about their relationship. The closer and stronger the relationship, the more people tend to touch. We always notice if a couple touches each other during an in-home interview. We also notice how closely they sit together. Our experience has been that couples that are in distress tend to sit the farthest apart and don't touch each other at all. In contrast, happier couples tend to sit closely and will occasionally touch each other.

Eyes

It has been said that the eyes are the window to the soul, and that statement may have more than a bit of truth to it. Our eyes reveal whom we like and what captures our attention. We tend to look more frequently at the people and things we like and find interesting, and we also tend to look at them for a longer duration. One can tell when people are in love because they look at each other for long periods of time. People who don't like one another will rarely engage in eye contact unless they are being openly confrontational. Interestingly, we betray our prejudices with our eyes. In a classic study on racial prejudice, researchers learned that those who are prejudiced against African Americans look at them for a shorter period of time during interviews than individuals who are not prejudiced (Dovidio et al. 1997). The interesting thing about this finding is that people were unaware that they were looking at one group for less time than the other. Thus, our eyes say all kinds of things about whom we like and whom we don't like.

In market research, we notice how long people look at products and services that we show them. The longer folks tend to look at things, the more they tend to be interested in them. The less they look at things, the less they tend to like them. We also notice how long people look at one another in a group discussion.

People tend to look at those whom they like and respect. In almost every focus group, one person may have a strong point of view that he shares with the group. The duration of time that people look at him tells me how much they share his point of view and whether they like him.

Eye behavior can also tell you a great deal about who the leader is in a group or who has influence in a relationship. Sometimes people will look at their husband or wife when they answer a question to confirm that they are saying the correct thing. Sometimes people even look to me when I am moderating a focus group to determine if they've said the right thing. I discourage them from looking to me for any type of affirmation because there is no right or wrong answer in market research.

Eye behavior also tells us about how cognitively complex an issue is for someone to discuss. Generally, when people access a memory or figure out an answer, they tend to look away. If I asked you right now to multiply two large numbers, you would probably look away to do the calculation and then come back to this page. The same is true for anything that we are figuring out or remembering. If I asked you to think of the names of several friends from third grade, you would probably look away to think about your memories from that time and the names of your friends. After you remember these names, you would then look back to this page. These eye behaviors are useful because the amount of time that people look away tells how close their answers are to the tops of their minds. If people have to look away to answer basic questions, such as where they grew up or what they do for a living, I begin to wonder if they are being entirely truthful.

Eyes Reveal Cognitive Complexity

The last thing that eye behavior reveals is whether something is emotionally difficult to discuss. People tend to look away when they are talking about something that they are ashamed of or that is embarrassing. They will also look away if something is difficult to discuss because it's emotionally evocative. Looking away allows people to gain control of their emotions, which is why people break eye contact. I watch eye behavior closely and notice if something seems difficult for a person to discuss. In those situations, I may redirect the conversation and come back to the topic later. I may also say that these things can be difficult to discuss as a way to reassure someone. By being sensitive to what a person is feeling about a conversation, we can learn more about her thoughts and feelings without making the situation uncomfortable for her.

Individual Gestures

Individual gestures are one of my favorite things to watch when respondents talk. There are two basic types of gestures: *emblems* and *illustrators*. Emblems are gestures that have a direct translation to a word or phrase. Most people within a culture will know the translation for these gestures. Examples of these emblems in American culture are the gestures for "Okay," "Be quiet," "Shame on you," "He's crazy," and so on. These are common gestures that most people understand. See the next pictures for examples of emblems.

Emblem for "Be Quiet"

Emblem for "Good" or "Okay"

The other type of gesture is an illustrator, which doesn't have a clear verbal translation and seems somewhat random at first glance. However, it can convey a great deal of meaning. Illustrators often reveal an image in someone's mind and his perceptions of the world. Some of the things that these gestures can convey are

- how things are grouped (e.g., brands, companies, types of products or services);
- how far apart things are (e.g., how closely aligned groups, people, ideas, brands are in someone's mind);
- where things are located in a physical space (e.g. how far away something is, where something is located in reference to something else);
- the shapes of objects;
- how large or small things or ideas are for a person;
- how we use something (e.g., an appliance);
- the order of things or the steps that are taken to achieve an outcome;
- to whom we are referring; and
- ideas or beliefs that are important to us.

Respondents gesture all the time, and they often tell us things that people don't even realize they're revealing. For example, companies often want to know how people group their products with those of competitors. When people are talking, they will often put similar brands in the same space. You can watch how closely they place them together to see which companies are perceived as most similar. Respondents will also gesture about how large or small they perceive a company or brand to be. They will also paint scenes in front of you with their hands, and if you look closely, you can see the images that they are visualizing in their minds. People will describe what things look like, how large they are, and what their shape is with their gestures. One of the best examples of this is to ask someone to give you directions and watch how she starts gesticulating about where you need to go. She is literally translating her view of your journey with her hands. The following photos show some examples of what gestures can convey.

Gesture Showing How Closely Two Brands Are Aligned

Gesture Showing the Size of an Idea

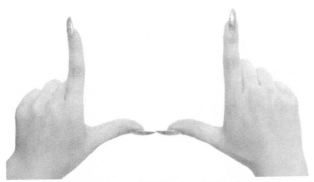

Gesture Showing Shape of a Product

Gestures also reveal how people use products. In some instances, we realized that respondents were dissatisfied with a product because they were using it incorrectly. Their gestures showed us how they used an appliance, and it became clear that some of them had not read the directions and were having problems. Respondents will also indicate the order in which they do things with gestures. They will lay out the first step, the second one, and so on. When people explain these things to us, we get a better understanding about all the things they need to do for certain activities like making certain types of foods or planning a vacation. What may seem so straightforward may not be so when you see all the steps that are necessary.

Respondents also reveal the people they are thinking about or the beliefs they hold most deeply through gestures. They reveal these things through subtle (and not so subtle) pointing. On more than one occasion, people will give an example and will subtly point to a person they believe represents that example. They don't think they're overtly pointing to anyone, and they don't even realize that they're betraying their view of that person. On some occasions, the person being referred to doesn't realize it either, but in other cases, it's more obvious. The other thing that respondents do is to motion toward themselves or point to their chest when talking about something that is very important to them or that is a deeply held conviction. I remember watching a politician on television, who pointed to his heart as he explained to the crowd, "This is something that we strongly believe." His gesture revealed that the issue was something in which *he* strongly believed. That same politician then pointed to the audience and said, "This is something that we need to do." His gestures said that it was something that he wanted the audience to do.

Respondents also tend to gesture more when they are confident or enthusiastic about something. If you watch people speak, you can see that the largest gestures tend to occur around the words or phrases that they are emphasizing in their speech. I always find it interesting to see what topics lead to gesturing. I once ran a workshop with businesspeople about reading nonverbal communication. I had the participants do an exercise in which they talked about various things and observed their partner's gestures. One man didn't have a partner, so I went over to do the exercise with him. He promptly told me that he never gestures, and he didn't—until we started talking about a topic that wasn't a part of the exercise. We started talking about his kids, and he started gesturing. Obviously, this was a topic about which he was very enthusiastic. People differ in the amount that they gesture, but most people will gesture a little bit when talking about something that is important to them.

Voice

The voice reveals many things. One thing it reveals is our emotions. People betray their emotions with the pitch, volume, and speed of their speech. For example, people tend to speak more slowly and to use lower pitches when they're sad. When people are happy, they tend to speak more quickly. Interestingly, people tend to use higher pitches when they're stressed. We are surprisingly able to read the emotions of speakers even if we cannot see them. The emotional states that we're most able to recognize are anger, happiness, boredom, interest, contempt, and sadness. Disgust and shame are harder to decode (Pittam & Scherer 1993; Banse & Scherer 1996).

Reading voices becomes important particularly when one is conducting in-depth telephone interviews. We know from researchers that one can tell another person's age, gender, and social class just from listening to her voice (Remland 2000). The voice can also reveal whether someone is an extrovert or an introvert. Extroverts tend to talk quickly, moderately loudly, and fluently, and tend to have longer utterances. Introverts, in contrast, tend to talk slowly, somewhat quietly, less fluently, and they speak in shorter utterances.

The voice also reveals when something is difficult to discuss or when it's cognitively complex. People tend to pause when they are either accessing a memory or figuring out an answer. The pause does the same thing that the eyes do when we look away to think about or remember something. People pause when trying to remember something that is not at the top of their minds. The other time that people pause is when they are having difficulty talking about something that is emotionally evocative for them. You can tell whether an issue is cognitively complex or difficult to discuss from observing the voice along with all of the other nonverbal behaviors.

Existence of Adaptors

Adaptors are those small, fidgety behaviors such as twirling a pen, rotating a ring, twisting one's hair, biting one's lip, or biting one's nails. People tend to have adaptors when they feel stressed or bored. Apparently, adaptors help us deal with our boredom or stress because they give us an outlet for our feelings and pent-up energy. The interesting thing about these behaviors is that we share them with other primates. When a higher-status primate walks into a lower-status primate's environment, the lower-status one starts to show adaptors (Maestripier et al. 1992). He may play with his fur or pick at a stick, and he looks surprisingly human when he does this.

Examples of Adaptors among Primates and Humans

Adaptors are useful things to watch because they reveal periods of stress or boredom. I watch for doodling in my focus groups because I know that if the conversation becomes relatively uninteresting, the number of adaptors in the room will increase. In some cases, this situation cannot be helped. However, it does let me know that people may not be listening intently to the discussion. The existence of adaptors also tells me that someone may be stressed about a topic. In some interviews I've had with respondents about financial services, they have started to show adaptors when they talk about the financial decisions they have made for their families. The fact that people were showing adaptors may have revealed that they were uncomfortable with some of the decisions they made.

Years ago, we did a study for a company about its website. We asked respondents to go onto two firms' websites (the company's website and a competitor's website) and do certain activities. We videotaped them while they were surfing, and we counted the number of adaptors that occurred while they were on each website. We then asked them to evaluate how user-friendly the websites were after they were finished. One website was much easier to navigate than the other. Respondents had many more adaptors when they were on the website that was difficult to navigate and very few adaptors on the easier website. We deduced the ease or difficulty of the websites just by counting the number of adaptors, and we were correct.

Putting It All Together

When we observe respondents in different research situations (e.g., in a home, in a store, in a focus-group facility), we observe all aspects of their nonverbal communication in addition to listening to what they have to say. Because everyone is different, there are some rules that we use when watching people. These rules are
- watch an individual for variations from her baseline;
- watch for variations from the normal situation; and
- watch for variations expressed toward different people.

Everyone is different, and some people are naturally more expressive than others. Thus, there is a baseline for every person. We watch variations from that baseline. If Katherine is naturally expressive and she tells me nonverbally that she loves the new model of car I've shown her, we take her natural expressivity into consideration. Her verbal and nonverbal behaviors say that she's pretty enthusiastic about a lot of things and that she's an extroverted woman. However, if Matthew is not particularly expressive and he becomes expressive after viewing an advertisement, his expressive behavior says something significant about the way the ad affected him. We also watch for variations from a particular norm. Certain situations call for a different level of expressivity, and groups create their own norms. If a focus group gets somewhat boisterous and high-spirited because it's occurring on a Friday afternoon, we watch for variations from that norm. Last, we watch for variations expressed toward different people. If Don has one reaction to Nancy Pelosi and another reaction to Donald Trump, that provides us with important information about his feelings about these individuals.

Through observing all the different aspects of PERCEIVE™, we watch for emotional reactions; ease or difficulty in talking about things; how complex issues are for people; how much people like or dislike one another; and how much they like or dislike the brands, products, and services that we show them. We also watch for deception and for behavior that tells us that the respondent is telling us what she thinks we want to hear. Sadly, the proliferation of the market-research industry has created a group of people who are professional research respondents. These people make a significant amount of money going from study to study—a practice that we abhor. The nonverbal indicators of deception are very useful to us in ferreting out these folks.

CHAPTER 8: ANALYZING QUALITATIVE DATA

Analyzing qualitative data is an art and a science. How does one do that? One of the major things that we do is to capture qualitative data with a template. The function of the template is to document the major findings from each interview so that we can compare the findings across individuals and determine if there are any patterns. We enter this information into an Excel spreadsheet.

The kinds of things we enter into the sheet include basic information about each respondent and anything that we want to compare (e.g., age, family structure). We will also provide information such as specific needs they have, what they're looking for, and how much of a product/service they have or need. The goal of capturing this information is to understand if certain groups tend to have different attitudes or certain preferences. For example, we recently did a study of small businesses, and we learned that those that had only been in business for a couple of years had very different attitudes and different needs than businesses that had been around for a longer period. Our client realized that they had to approach these businesses very differently when selling their website service.

Thus, analyzing qualitative data involves actually counting, plotting and taking this open-ended information and putting numbers around it. And we do this using our hypotheses. How many women prefer the new product over the previous one? We start counting. Are men and women similar or different in which features they like? We count. And do older respondents differ from younger ones. Again, we count. We don't present numbers as the output, but we do have a sense from this exercise what's happening in the data.

When we do shop-alongs, we like to plot how the respondent moved through the store. Let's take the example of a grocery store. If we want to understand typical shopping patterns, we will record where people typically went and what paths they followed. This information will provide us with an overview of how people shop with a map of their typical route. This technique can be a useful way to capture how people typically navigate an environment and can enable one to compare certain groups. Perhaps people with kids tend to take a different route than those who don't. That kind of information can be very useful.

Numeric data can also help bring people's decisions to life. For example, when we test different ads, we always ask people to rate how appealing an ad is on a scale of one to ten where one is "not at all appealing" and a ten is "extremely appealing." We then ask people to write what they think the message is for each ad. We retain this information because it helps us to understand what people really mean when they say an ad is appealing to them and what message they received from it.

We also use frameworks to explain behavior. As a social psychologist, I often consult theoretical frameworks to identify what is causing the behavior that's occuring. For example, we had a banking client that wanted to understand why people continually bounce checks month after month and year after year. These are individuals who overdraft their checking accounts and continually pay high fees. We interviewed chronic overdrafters to understand what leads them to keep making this mistake over and over.

What we learned was that these individuals don't see themselves as chronic overdrafters and tend to view each overdraft occurrence as an isolated event. When they bounce a check or overdraft their debit card, they tend to view the experience as the result of bad luck that's unlikely to happen again. Both of these attitudes are found in social psychology—one is called *unrealistic optimism* and the other is called the *self-serving bias*. Unrealistic optimism is essentially the belief that positive future events are more likely to occur for us than negative future events. Most people see the future as fairly rosy. Self-serving bias is the tendency for us to excuse our failures and take credit for our successes. In general, we see ourselves as better than the average person. Taken together, these two cognitive biases explain why our chronic overdrafters continue to bounce checks. Once we saw these biases, we put together this framework to explain the phenomenon:

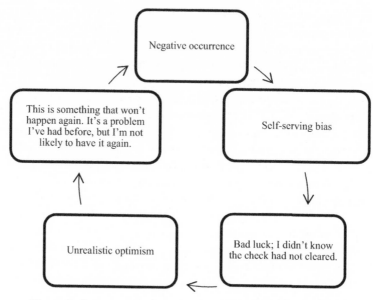

Figure 8: Framework for Explaining Chronic Overdrafting

As you can see in the above figure, when an overdraft occurred, the self-serving bias kicked in, and the person justified the overdraft as due to some unforeseeable piece of bad luck, like a payment for them being late. At that point, the unrealistic optimism bias kicked in, and the person further reasoned that this event was a somewhat isolated incident that wasn't likely to occur again. These two cognitive biases caused these individuals to continue to overdraft their accounts.

Another example of how we can use frameworks to make sense of behavior occurs with consumers' use of brands and services. We recently did a project for a major gym membership provider. They wanted to understand why they weren't retaining many of their members. We interviewed members who had left who represented different tenures of membership. We discussed each aspect of the experience: from joining and initial interactions, through various interactions, until the decision to leave. When we looked at the stories that emerged, we saw a common pattern that fit the ABCDE model of relationships by Levinger (1983). We learned that there was often a specific event that caused a deterioration of the relationship with the brand and that this company was not adequately addressing their members in terms of rebuilding the relationship when there was a problem.

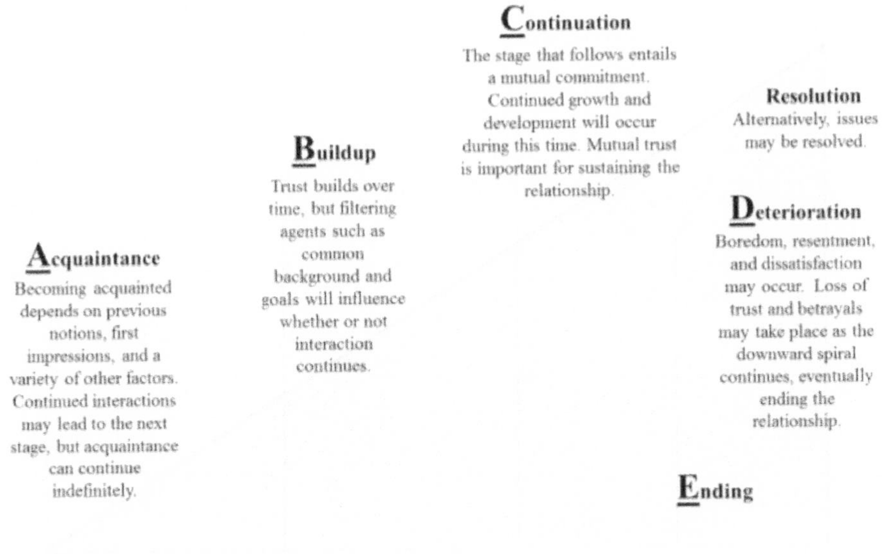

Continuation

The stage that follows entails
a mutual commitment.
Continued growth and
development will occur
during this time. Mutual trust
is important for sustaining the
relationship.

Resolution

Alternatively, issues
may be resolved.

Buildup

Trust builds over
time, but filtering
agents such as
common
background and
goals will influence
whether or not
interaction
continues.

Deterioration

Boredom, resentment,
and dissatisfaction
may occur. Loss of
trust and betrayals
may take place as the
downward spiral
continues, eventually
ending the
relationship.

Acquaintance

Becoming acquainted
depends on previous
notions, first
impressions, and a
variety of other factors.
Continued interactions
may lead to the next
stage, but acquaintance
can continue
indefinitely.

Ending

Figure 9: Levinger's Model of Relationships

Text Analysis or "Digital Listening"

Another tool that we use to analyze qualitative data is text analysis, which allows us to analyze the frequency of words, concepts, and linguistics. You can conduct this analysis on focus-group and interview transcripts to understand what people say and how they say it. You can also use this type of analysis on websites' postings. We recently ran a text analysis on online consumer reviews of three cellular companies. We wanted to determine if there were differences in the experience of the customers of these companies who post reviews on the internet. We pulled 60,252 words for the three brands (at least 20,000 per brand) and then analyzed the common concepts and words people used to describe them. All reviews were from the year 2018 and were vetted to ensure that they were written by real people who had actually used the company. In addition, we reviewed the posts to ensure they were cellular customers so that we'd know we were comparing cell customers across the three providers.

The first analysis we conduct simply looks at which words people use the most. This type of analysis is often shown in word clouds, shown below. The size of the word indicates its frequency. Thus, words that are larger occurred more often for that company.

Figure 10: Brand 1 Word Cloud

Figure 11: Brand 2 Word Cloud

Figure 12: Brand 3 Word Cloud

As the word clouds show, the words *charge/fee* and *call* appear prominently in discussions of all three of these companies. However, there are more references to *pay/payments* among Brand 3 reviewers than among users of the other companies. The words *supervisor/manager* appear more for Brand 1 customers than for other customers. All three groups use the word *store* and *phone bill*, but Brand 3 customers mention their bill the most.

The next analysis is in terms of common concepts that appear in posts to determine if there are differences in what people are saying about these companies. Concepts are an amalgamation of words and phrases that express the same idea. For example, *easy* could comprise the words and phrases *easy, not difficult, easy to do, simple to learn, effortless*, etc. We conduct a statistical analysis to see whether the frequency of these concepts is similar or different among the three companies. We use a chi-square analysis, which assumes that there will be an equal usage of these words/concepts by company. If the result is statistically significant, it means that there are differences in the number of mentions of that concept across the three providers. Below is a sample of what we found in this analysis.

Concept	Brand 1	Brand 2	Brand 3	Statistically Significantly Different?
Switched to Brand 3	0%	17%	83%	Yes
Friendly/Nice Service	22%	22%	56%	Yes
Love the company	4%	33%	63%	Yes
Unlimited Plan	12%	61%	27%	Yes
Unlimited Data	24%	61%	15%	Yes
Online Chat with Customer Support	25%	65%	11%	Yes
Hours on the Phone	49%	18%	33%	Yes
False Promises	56%	21%	24%	Yes
Supervisor/Manager	52%	12%	36%	Yes

Table 11: Analysis of Concepts and Keywords

As you can see in the table above, Brand 3 customers were more likely than other cell customers to mention that they had switched to that company, to talk about friendly service they had experienced, and to say they loved the company. In contrast, Brand 2 cellular customers were more likely to mention unlimited data, their unlimited plan, and online chatting with customer support than other customers. Brand 1 customers, in contrast, were more likely to mention spending hours on the phone talking to customer service, false promises and to mention supervisors or managers they interacted with as compared to other cellular customers.

In addition to analyzing what people said, we analyzed how they said it. Some of the major analyses that we do are based on linguistic work of Pennebaker (2011). We analyze linguistic properties such as the following:

- cognitive processes, which are defined as active thinking about an experience
  - "I understand why ..."
  - "I realize that ..."
- causation, which involves drawing cause and effect
  - "The reason I like it is because ..."
  - "It depends on whether ..."
- certainty, which indicates speaking with definite or absolute language
  - "You absolutely cannot ..."
  - "It's always like this ..."

- positive emotional expressions
  - "I love this ..."
  - "This is great."
- negative emotional expressions
  - "I hate that ..."
  - "It's frustrating ..."
- past tense
  - "I used to ...
- present tense
  - "Currently ..."
- future tense
  - "I plan to ..."

Concept	Brand 1	Brand 2	Brand 3	Statistically Significantly Different?
Money	34%	30%	36%	Yes
Feeling	23%	31%	46%	Yes
Positive Emotion	30%	34%	36%	Yes

Table 12: Linguistic Analysis

As you can see from this analysis, there weren't many differences in the language of reviewers. We usually see more differences in our studies. In this case, Brand 3 customers were more likely to discuss feelings than the customers of the other two companies. And Brand 2 and Brand 3 customers were more likely to express positive emotions in their reviews versus Brand 1 cell customers.

Another analysis that we conduct with this qualitative data is a correspondence analysis, which identifies variables that are most uniquely associated with each company. In this analysis, you can see that the variables most uniquely corresponding to Brand 3 are payments, phone bill, switching companies. Brand 2 is more associated with plans and coverage. And Brand 1 seems to be most associated with spending hours on the phone with their customer-service reps.

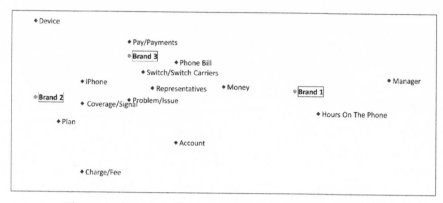

Figure 13: Correspondence Analysis of Cellular Provider Plans

CHAPTER 9: ANALYZING QUANTITATIVE DATA

The way that data is analyzed can make the difference between a project that just provides information and a study that offers real insight. Our approach to data analysis is to start with our hypotheses and to test these ideas rather than to expect data to magically tell us a story. There are two schools of thought in the market research world. One school advocates doing a variety of analyses that aren't driven by any underlying hypotheses and to see what pops up. The other school advocates a hypothesis-driven approach, in which you test your hypotheses about a market and learn what really drives it. We clearly subscribe to the school of thought that tests hypotheses, and I'll show you why this approach often works much better than just expecting the data to magically provide an answer.

Hypothesis-Driven Analyses

As already described in a previous chapter, we begin a study by understanding a client's hypotheses about their customers and markets. Let's imagine that we're doing a project for a new type of fitness app. We have the following hypotheses:

- Gender hypothesis: women will be more likely than men to purchase this new app.
- Age hypothesis: younger consumers will be more likely than older consumers to purchase this new app.
- Income hypothesis: higher-income consumers will be more likely to purchase this new app than lower-income consumers.

There are likely to be quite a few hypotheses that an organization generates. These hypotheses will in turn lead to more hypotheses. If these were the only three hypotheses that were identified, we could also say that young, high-income women would be most likely to purchase this app. The group that would be the least likely to buy it's hypothesized to be older, low-income men.

We then create a set of cross-tabulations that specifically tests these assertions. We divide the data by all three of these categories. We can look at the data for each group and determine if our hypotheses are supported or not. The best way to analyze these results is to conduct t-tests comparing each group's results. Thus, we can compare whether women are significantly more likely than men to purchase this app, whether low-income people are less likely to purchase than high-income people, and so forth. This approach tends to lead to other hypotheses, which in turn lead to other analyses. So, if we find that women are more likely to purchase this app we may hypothesize that they like the fact that it's new technology. We may do further cross-tabulations to look at people who appreciate that this app is cutting-edge technology, so we can determine if these things are related to gender. The result is that we have a clear set of analyses that are directed by the early thinking we did when we commenced this project. These analyses allow us to eventually tell a story about the findings.

So, what's wrong with the approach that lets the data speak for itself? The problem with just letting the data speak for itself is that sometimes it doesn't. Data doesn't magically appear with interesting results. We need to divide it, subdivide it, and ask questions of it in order to fully understand a market. On many occasions, people set up cross-tabulations without any sense of why one group might differ from another and without underlying explanations of why these differences would exist. Early in my career, I worked at a company with a man who loved statistics and who liked to throw all the variables from a study into different analyses because he assumed that something interesting would appear. He would do correlations and cluster analyses with tons of variables, hoping to find some magical answer. The result was often reams of paper with tons of numbers and no clear story about what the data said. He ended up becoming very frustrated and often couldn't provide great value to his clients.

Analyses to Determine What Predicts Perceptions and Behavior

Sometimes clients want to know what predicts purchasing behavior or what determines certain perceptions. The only way to accurately identify if something has an effect is to use an *experimental design*. An experimental design takes an *independent variable* and manipulates it in some way, measuring the effect of this manipulation on a *dependent variable*. When the only thing that changes is the independent variable, any effect on a dependent variable is due to that independent variable. Thus, you can measure the effect of color on the attractiveness of a specific car by manipulating only the color of a car and measuring perceptions of the attractiveness to see if color has an effect. You might learn that color has a large effect on perceptions of a Prius and that the car is much more attractive when it's shown in unusual colors.

We used an experimental design for a study that we conducted for the American Academy of Cosmetic Dentistry. They wanted to learn whether one's smile influences perceptions of attractiveness and personality. To determine whether a smile influences perceptions, we took pictures of eight individuals (four women and four men) and varied the smile. We used Photoshop so that the picture of the person was exactly the same—same clothing, same hair, and same facial expression. The only thing that was different was the smile. Each person was pictured two times. In one picture, the person had white, straight teeth (the beautiful smile condition); in the other picture, the teeth were less white and not as straight (the regular smile condition). See the next picture for an example. We used a complicated research design in which everyone saw pictures of people that either had a beautiful smile or a regular smile. However, *no respondent saw the same person with both smiles.*

"Regular smile" on the left and "Beautiful smile" on the right

Respondents rated the pictured individuals on their attractiveness, intelligence, happiness, and career success, and also on how friendly, interesting, kind, wealthy, popular with the opposite sex, and how sensitive to other people they appeared. We then analyzed the data to determine if the type of smile made a difference when people had the beautiful smile instead of the regular smile. Because the only thing that varied was the smile, any differences in perceptions were due to the smile. We were amazed to learn that when people have a beautiful smile with white and straight teeth, people perceive them as more attractive, intelligent, happy, successful in their career, friendly, interesting, kind, wealthy, popular with the opposite sex, and sensitive to other people than when they don't have such a smile (Beall 2007). This study is an excellent example of how one can use an experimental design to determine what predicts specific perceptions.

In cases when one cannot do an experiment because you can't control the major variables as easily as in the study above, you can learn which variables are related by using a correlation analysis. You can determine if gender, age, or attitudes are highly related to purchasing a new cell-phone by correlating these variables with actual purchases or respondents' stated intention to purchase the cell phone. Low correlations indicate that two things are not related to one another and that one variable is not related to the other. High correlations indicate the opposite. Thus, we might find a high correlation between income and propensity to purchase a new cell phone. As income increases, the likelihood of purchasing a new cell-phone also increases. However, correlations don't indicate causation. Just because two things are highly correlated doesn't mean that one causes the other. Having a high income doesn't cause one to be interested in purchasing a new cell phone; it's more complicated than that.

Analyses to Determine the Major Segments in a Market

Another question that organizations want to answer is what the major segments are in a market. They want to understand which specific groups are most likely to purchase their product and why. Organizations want to learn how large these groups are, what they are like demographically, and how to communicate effectively with them. By identifying market segments, organizations can determine which groups they want to expend resources on and which ones will be most likely to respond. Segmentations are a way of describing a market as well as a way of providing direction for an organization's marketing efforts.

We are strong advocates of segmentations that are customized for a specific company's product or service. We believe that unless a segmentation is based on data that's collected for a specific category, it will not be useful. We've never seen a segmentation that is valuable for driving major strategic decisions that wasn't created exclusively for that organization. We've seen numerous examples of marketing executives buying segmentations that can be purchased by anyone, including their competitors, and that ultimately provide little or no value. So if you want to know about the segments in the dog food market, conduct a segmentation study specifically about dog food and the major brands that play there. Don't buy a secondary segmentation that was designed for all businesses (often based on psychographics) and expect to figure out the segments of dog-food buyers.

Our approach to segmentation is first to define which variables are most critical for the organization. We determine this variable based on how the organization will use the segmentation. If the company is trying to predict which groups prefer specific brands, then the critical variable is which brand each respondent has bought or intends to buy. If the company wants to separate those who spend a lot from those who don't, then the critical variable is the amount purchased. Once we determine the critical variable, we will identify which variables are most related to it and why. After identifying the variables that are highly related, we will usually do a cluster analysis or we'll combine them to create segments.

For example, let's say we're interested in cell phone usage and that we want to create a segmentation for a cell phone company (Carrier A). Let's imagine that our client cares most about identifying people who use a lot of data and who are most likely to purchase their brand of service. They want to offer certain packages to these individuals. We might do an analysis that determines that age is highly related to data usage and that younger consumers use data the most. We might determine that what predicts brand usage among young users is the cell phone service their parents are using. What might predict that brand usage among slightly older users is the brand their friends are using. We might end up with a segmentation that looks like this:

Segment 1: under-twenty-five-year-olds whose parents use Carrier A
Segment 2: under-twenty-five-year-olds whose parents use other carriers
Segment 3: thirty- to forty-year-olds whose friends use Carrier A
Segment 4: thirty- to forty-year-olds whose friends use other carriers
Segment 5: forty- to fifty-year-olds
Segment 6: fifty-one- to sixty-four-year-olds
Segment 7: sixty-five-plus-year-olds

We could then profile these groups to determine if their behavior and attitudes are what we predicted. Let's assume that our predictions are borne out in the data and that Segment 1 has the highest data usage and the greatest loyalty toward Carrier A, followed by Segment 3. Thus, the highest-priority segment would be Segment 1, followed by Segment 3. In this case, the company has clear direction about which segments are most valuable to them and which ones they should target first. Additional profiling of these groups in terms of their attitudes, usage, and desired services will allow the company to be able to offer data services that these segments want and to communicate with them in ways that are productive.

Thinking about how a segmentation will be used down the road is a critical part of the analysis process. Many years ago, I worked for a consulting firm that used to do segmentations for Regional Bell Operating Companies (RBOCs, or local phone companies like Atlantic Bell, Ameritech, and Pacific Bell) who wanted to enter the long-distance market. Deregulation was in its infancy, and there were special rules about how phone companies could use consumer data. The local phone companies weren't allowed to use their own data to target customers for long-distance service. Thus, to assign every household in the area to a segment, we needed to use data that could be purchased from external data vendors. We created an algorithm that could be used to assign everyone to a specific segment. After assigning all households in a geographic area to segments, the company intended to contact people in specific segments with an offer to purchase long distance service. Thus, when we created the segments, we had to stick to variables that could be bought from the large data vendors. Thinking through how the segments would be used and what the data constraints were for these companies was extremely important and ended up yielding a segmentation that they used to go to market.

Sometimes a segmentation needs to serve different purposes for different groups in an organization. We did such a segmentation for an educational foundation. We learned that there were two ways of viewing this organization's customers. One part of the organization viewed customers in terms of the type of organizations that bought the educational materials. The other part of the organization viewed the customers in terms of how much they spent on the educational materials. Thus, we needed to create a segmentation that would address the needs of both of these client groups. We achieved this objective by identifying segments that overlapped. The eventual solution allowed the client to look at the segments as either organizational segments or as value segments. As you can see in the figure below, the segmentation looks somewhat like a Rubik's Cube, and you can look at the segments in different ways. By addressing how the segmentation would be used by two groups down the road, we created a solution that was very useful.

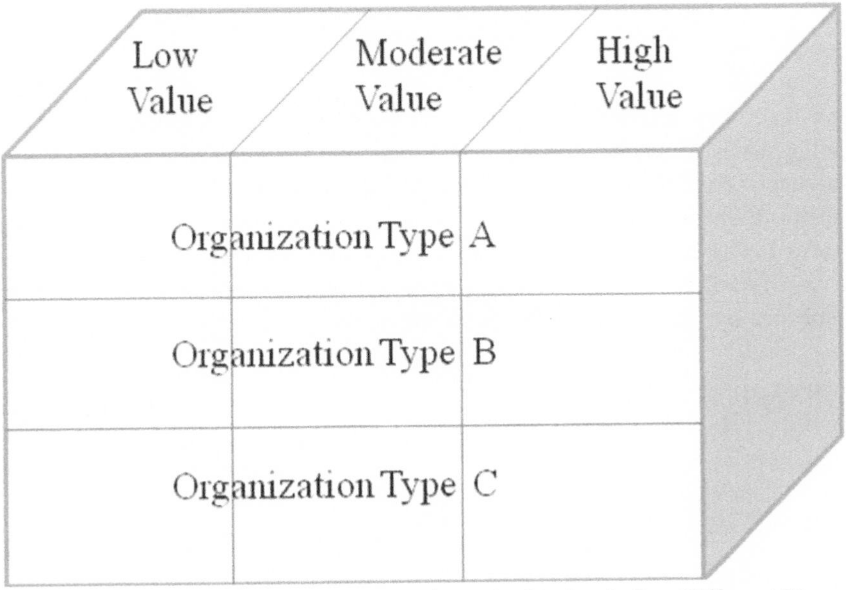

Low Value	Moderate Value	High Value
Organization Type	A	
Organization Type	B	
Organization Type	C	

Figure 14: Segmentation That Views the Market in Two Different Ways

Analyses to Determine the Best Configuration for a Product or Service

Organizations often want to identify what the best configuration is for their product or service. For example, car manufacturers want to know what kinds of features to put on a luxury car that will create the greatest demand for it. They also want to know which features are most valued, so they can create the vehicle that people are willing to pay a great deal to own. So how do you do that? We use conjoint/choice analysis to identify the best product configuration for certain groups of people or for a market overall. They enable us to figure out what the potential demand is for a large number of product configurations. Let's imagine that we're trying to design a cell phone. We first define the product attributes and then the levels of these attributes. We might come up with the following:

- Screen size
- Provider of cellular service
- Length of contract
- Brand of cell phone
- Amount of memory
- Weight
- Price
- Etc.

We then show different configurations of cell phones to respondents and ask them how likely they would be to purchase each one. The number of cell phones and the particular configurations are determined by a model that we eventually use after the data is collected to simulate many configurations, including ones that we have not tested. The result is a simulator in which you can see customer demand for any type of cell phone that uses the attributes and levels that were tested. An example of a simulator is shown in the screen capture below.

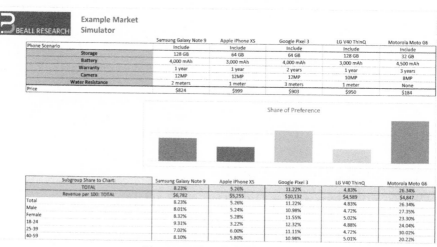

Figure 15: Example Simulator

96

We can also use the simulator to optimize the product in order to gain a certain market share. Optimizing products and services is an important part of product development. Organizations can use these simulators to see which configuration would compete best with the products that are currently available. They can also optimize pricing to obtain a certain market share, see how adding a new product or removing a current one would impact their share and simulate potential competitor products to see how well they would compete with them. These tools are invaluable because they have so many different applications. You could use this tool to optimize the layout of your lunchroom. We know of a case in which a large nonprofit organization used conjoint analysis to identify the best positioning and supporting statements for a national advertising campaign.

Analyses to Determine Which Product Attributes Are Most Important

Another type of analysis that we conduct is designed to identify which features of a product are most important to one's satisfaction with a product/service. This type of research is very useful when a product or service has been out in the market for a while and a company wants to understand what features of the product have the greatest impact on overall satisfaction with the product/service and what would lead people to buy it again.

For example, let's imagine that a major hotel chain wants to understand what causes their guests to be highly satisfied and likely to return. They need to know where they should invest their money to get the greatest return. Should they invest in updating the fitness room, the food selection, the comfort of the beds, the desk areas, or the entertainment on their TVs? They can measure current satisfaction with each of these areas and then determine what impact these areas have on likelihood to return to the hotel when people are satisfied or dissatisfied with them. Through a regression analysis, they can determine that for certain types of guests, the areas that have the greatest impact on satisfaction vary and that these are the areas they should invest in if they want to have the greatest return on their investment. See the table below for an example of the type of output one could obtain.

Business Traveler	Percent Highly Satisfied	Leisure Travelers	Percent Highly Satisfied
#1 Internet Connection	74%	#1 Entertainment on TV	35%
#2 Food Selection	34%	#2 Food Selection	44%
#3 Desk Area	82%	#3 Comfort of Bed	56%
#4 Fitness Area	24%	#4 Internet Connection	88%
#5 Comfort of Bed	46%	#5 Pool	68%

Table 13: Attributes That Have Greatest Impact on Likelihood to Return to Hotel and Current Satisfaction

In the above table, it's clear that the top five attributes for the hotel that have the greatest impact on satisfaction are different for business travelers compared to leisure ones. For business travelers, the areas of lowest satisfaction among the attributes that have the greatest impact are the food selection, fitness area, and comfort of the beds. These would be the areas to invest in if one is trying to increase satisfaction and likelihood to return among these guests. And among leisure travelers, it's clear that the entertainment on TV, the food selection, and the comfort of the beds are the areas that are highly influential for this group and for whom the satisfaction is the lowest. If one were trying to appeal to both groups, it would be wise to invest in new mattresses and a better food selection.

Brand Tracking and the Impact of Advertising

Another major analysis that we perform helps companies understand the impact of their advertising on perceptions of their brand and on likelihood to purchase it. Many practitioners believe that advertising leads to increased awareness and that increased awareness leads to greater consideration, which leads to purchasing. We have conducted analyses to identify what variables actually lead to purchasing, and we found that for some brands, increasing awareness of the company doesn't lead to increased likelihood of buying that product or service. Instead, we found that for well-known companies, the level of familiarity that people have with a brand and specific perceptions of that brand such as "high quality" or "good value for the money" are important predictors of purchasing.

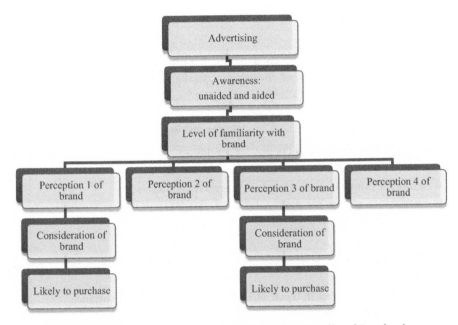

Figure 16: Model for Major Company about What Predicted Purchasing

Once we know what is most predictive of purchasing, we can begin to track those variables closely and determine how the brand is doing compared with its competitors. The vertical line in the figure below represents the launch of a new ad campaign and the tracking of the perceptions of that brand that were most related to purchasing it.

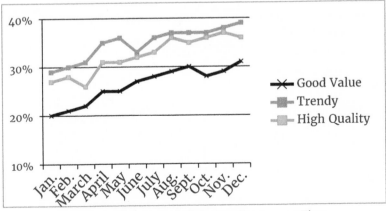

Figure 17: Tracking of Major Predictors over Time

Other Analyses

There are a variety of statistical analyses that can be used to gain insight. The table below shows some examples of the major questions that you can answer and the suggested statistical tools.

Example Question	Suggested Statistical Tool
How related are two variables (e.g., how related are gender and income)?	Correlation
Which set of things is most related to a variable (e.g., how are age, gender, and education related to income)?	Regression analysis
Are there significant differences between groups?	t-test, analysis of variance (ANOVA, F-test)
Do specific groups differ in terms of certain attitudes or behaviors?	Multivariate analysis of variance (MANOVA)
Are preferences for products or services similar or different than what would be expected by chance?	Chi-squared analysis
What is the underlying structure of a set of attitudes?	Factor analysis
What are the natural groups in a market?	Cluster analysis, Latent Class, CHAID
What is the optimal configuration for a product or service?	Conjoint, Discrete Choice Modeling
What are the most important needs, benefits, barriers, or attributes?	MaxDiff
What is the optimal lineup of products or services?	TURF, Conjoint

Table 14: Example Questions and Suggested Statistical Tool

CHAPTER 10: INTERPRETING RESULTS AND GOING BEYOND THE DATA

Often, market researchers assume that the data is the answer. Approximately 53 percent of people prefer this product, so that's the one that should be launched, right? Well, it might seem like the right product, but it might not be the best one for that company. So, if you can't just go by the data, how do you interpret results in a way that's useful? One of the best examples of this situation occurred early in my career when I was working with a brilliant consultant who ended up becoming a top executive at an ad agency in New York. We worked together on research for an online travel agency. He asked consumers what kind of name they would like for this travel agency, and the consumers tended to give pedestrian names such as TravelAgency.com and BookTravel.com. He then floated some names in front of these folks to get their reactions. Names that were fairly straightforward and somewhat boring tended to be liked the most. However, one name that was somewhat different and offbeat generated a mixed reaction. Some consumers liked it, and others hated it. The consultant recommended that the online company go with that name because it evoked a response. He wanted a name that would get a reaction—whether positive or negative. The online travel agency went with the offbeat name, and it's one of the most memorable names in that industry. That name is Orbitz.

Interpreting research results isn't just about selecting the concept with the highest score or with the greatest percentage of respondents who like it. It's about looking deeper into the research and asking several questions. What are respondents really saying when they give something a high score? Does that mean that's the one they understood better than the others, or is that the one that they found the most believable? What are respondents really reacting to when they give us their feedback? Do they like the catchphrases and the graphics, or are they responding to some overarching idea that grabs them? By looking a little deeper at what people are telling us, we can begin to understand what is really occurring. In the Orbitz example, respondents were saying that they liked names that fit with the service. They wanted a name that they could understand. The travel company's ad agency, however, wanted a name that communicated new and different and that was memorable. Thus, when they evaluated consumers' responses to the names, they listened to the strength of the reactions to the names rather than whether consumers liked them just because they were easy to understand.

When doing research, it's important to keep in mind that the evaluation criteria that consumers use may be different from the ones we use to help an organization. We did research for a major mattress manufacturer that was selecting an ad agency. It decided to put the materials of two agencies up against each other to see which agency was better. Let's call these Agencies A and B. The consumers claimed that they liked Agency A's materials better than B's. The reason they liked A's materials was because they were colorful and pleasant to look at. Agency B's materials were not as colorful or as attractive. However, when we dug more deeply into their responses, consumers told us that Agency B had a more innovative idea and that it was very alluring to them, but the materials turned them off. This mattress manufacturer realized that having a big idea was the major differentiator between ads, and they eventually selected Agency B. It turned out to be an excellent decision for them.

As a general rule, we shouldn't look to respondents to make business decisions. We don't just take whatever consumers prefer and recommend that as the answer. Interpreting market research in this way is naïve. We look at the reasons that something is preferred and make recommendations that make sense for the organization. When testing new products and services, we consider:

- How well does this product/service fit with this brand?
- How well could this company execute this product/service?
- Does this new product or service require a high level of advertising support to be successful?

On so many occasions, we've identified a winning product, but the company couldn't execute it well or couldn't provide the level of marketing support it required. One of my favorite clients is a company that puts very little money into national advertising, and its innovative products never get the exposure they deserve. People typically will not buy new, innovative products unless they're aware of them and have been educated about their benefits. Sadly, this company doesn't do either of these things well. The result is that the innovative products it has created never sell as well as they should, given our research results.

Reporting Results and Telling a Story

After the data from a study has been collected, some market researchers take the discussion guide or a survey and then parrot back each finding for each section of the study. The result is a compendium of information and little direction on how to interpret it or what to do as a result. The information is then put on a shelf somewhere and pulled out when someone asks about that particular study. I've seen these books in some of my clients' offices, and I marvel at the wasted time, money, and paper. What is the point of gathering information just for the sake of having it? Information isn't useful unless it can be used to make major decisions.

When I first began my career in this field, my mentor asked me to put the words "So what?" on the wall in front of my desk. He instructed me to look at those words every time I looked at data and then to integrate that thinking into my reports. I remember being irritated with him because it seemed like the information should be enough, but it wasn't. Because I was trained in a consulting firm, we were coached to look at data as a means to help a business rather than as mere information. I still look at research results that way. When I design questionnaires or conduct focus groups, I instinctively ask my clients, "If you knew that information, what would you do with that knowledge?" Knowing something is great, but only if you can act on it. There is very little point to asking a question if the information can't be used.

Because we take a strategic approach to market research, reporting of results follows all the work that we've done since the beginning of the project. We outline the questions that we were trying to answer and then address each question. We explain the reasons that we found each answer (why people think or behave the way they do) and what the implications of those answers are for the organization. We then outline our recommendations given these results. Our recommendations may sometimes be contentious, but they follow the strategic process that we believe so strongly in using. Our reports typically follow this format and tell a clear story that provides specific answers.

- objectives of this research
- major questions we were trying to answer
- answer to question 1

- o reasons for findings
- o implications
- answer to question 2
  - o reasons for finding
  - o implications
- major implications of findings
- recommendations

CHAPTER 11: COMMON PITFALLS IN MARKET RESEARCH

As a professional who has bought and sold market research for 25 years, I am well acquainted with the common pitfalls that occur in this practice. I've seen mistakes by some of my competitors and by some of my clients. Sadly, I've also made a few of my own mistakes along the way. The objective of this chapter is to review some of the major pitfalls to avoid.

Measuring Everything

Early in my career, I wanted to please my clients, so when they decided to add another section to a questionnaire, I agreed. I came to regret my decision when the survey came back and we had measured so many things superficially, but we hadn't gone into depth on anything. We couldn't explore anything to the level that we needed and were unable to provide our clients much insight. Organizations often want to maximize the money they spend on research, so they throw as much content as possible into a study. The result is a superficial understanding of many things. This type of research is often not particularly valuable. Sometimes, however, superficiality cannot be helped. No matter how many times you explain that a superficial understanding does not lead to results that can drive strategic decisions, the client somehow knows better. You end up with a questionnaire or a discussion guide that provides a little bit of information about everything possible.

Making Questionnaires Too Long

Another major problem with many surveys is that they are just too long. Long surveys tend to cause respondent boredom and fatigue. Although an organization might want to know every possible attitude toward its product, respondents often don't find such in-depth exploration particularly interesting. After they have answered the fiftieth question about how they think and feel about toothpaste, they are bored. In many cases, respondents have never thought about this category to the level that the questionnaire is written, and that can be fatiguing.

If questionnaires are perceived by respondents as too arduous or too boring, respondents tend to quit them, and the results can be biased. The group that eventually finishes the survey may be a small sample of respondents who are the most interested in the category or are completing the survey for some type of incentive (e.g., money or points for completion). If you only survey the people who are the most interested in a product and you are testing usage and attitudes, you might be surprised to learn that the average survey respondent uses a particular product more often than you expected. The results may not be indicative of usage among the larger population because you have only surveyed those highly involved respondents who completed your questionnaire. The less-involved folks got bored and decided not to finish the survey, so their attitudes and usage will never be known. In addition, if you are testing reactions to a client's potential new service, highly involved respondents should be more interested in that service. Thus, the forecasted purchase of this service will be overestimated.

We conducted an analysis of numerous surveys that ranged in length from ten minutes to forty minutes in order to determine if our beliefs were correct. Our analysis included thousands of respondents across a variety of topics. We analyzed the number of gibberish responses we received to open-ended questions, and we also looked at the proportion of people who "straight-lined," which is when respondents enter the same number into a rating scale over and over again—an indication that are not paying attention to the survey and just want to be finished with it. It's also an indication of poor data, particularly when two contradictory opinions are endorsed equally. We found that when a questionnaire was longer than twenty minutes, the amount of straight-lining and gibberish answers we received increased dramatically.

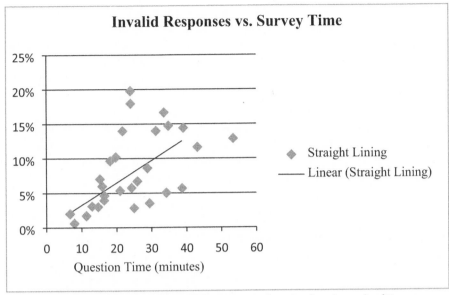

Figure 18: Percentage of Invalid Responses Received vs. Length of Survey

Insufficient Qualitative Research before Launching Surveys

In the consulting firm where I first learned how to do market research, we were taught to *always* pretest our quantitative surveys with individual interviews. We would design our surveys and then recruit individuals to come into a facility to take the survey in front of us. We would walk through every question with them and determine how they interpreted each question and every response. We would identify if any questions were unclear and if the response categories were appropriate for each question. I can honestly say that all of the surveys we launched using this approach produced the highest-quality data.

I am definitely a proponent of this approach, but sometimes there isn't enough time in the schedule to pretest surveys in this way. However, if enough qualitative work has been done to establish a thorough understanding of the product or service, we can use our qualitative research findings to design excellent surveys. There are several reasons why conducting qualitative research, such as individual interviews or focus groups, is important before designing surveys. Excellent qualitative research allows us to become knowledgeable about a category, and we learn the reasons people buy something. We also learn about the major attitudes people have about a brand and its competitors. We also learn how respondents talk about a product and the terminology they use. If we use terminology that is unfamiliar to respondents or refer to thoughts and feelings that don't capture their experiences, people will become frustrated with the survey and stop taking it. Terminology is particularly important. We have done many studies for pharmaceutical companies that are often surprised to learn that patients and physicians will refer to a disease very differently than they do. Even physicians sometimes use incorrect terminology. If we had designed a survey using the pharmaceutical company's terms, there would have been a great deal of confusion on the part of patients and physicians.

Relying on Respondents to Solve a Business Problem

One of the worst uses of market research involves having respondents solve a company's business problems. Expecting respondents to figure out what new products and services a business should offer, asking them to write ad copy, or figuring out how to save a business is a mistake. Respondents are not any more creative or insightful than the rest of us. Great researchers and marketers take market-research findings and use them as a tool to find the answer to a business problem. Respondents don't usually give us the answers directly.

One of the most frustrating projects I ever worked on involved an association that wanted to help its members figure out what new services it could offer its customers. This association approached us and asked if we would interview the customers of their members to learn what additional services the association members could offer their customers to make more money. We strongly recommended against using market research for this objective. We were concerned that these customers wouldn't know what else they wanted to buy from these members and might be uninterested in spending more money. The association resisted our advice and decided to forge ahead with the project. We interviewed several customers and asked them what else they would like to buy from these members. They told us one of two things: either they didn't want to buy anything else, or they couldn't think of anything else for these members to sell them. We were asking too much of them. They couldn't solve the business problems of these members any better than the association.

If you want to use market research to answer these types of strategic questions, the best approach is to put options in front of respondents and get their reactions.

Instead of asking respondents what services they want, I advocate putting potential services in front of them. By understanding their reactions to these potential ideas, we can begin to see patterns in what they want. We can identify what they like about each offering and then combine them into a service that they would be likely to buy. Similarly, if you need to understand how to communicate the attributes of a product, put some descriptions in front of respondents and then discern what concepts, words, and phrases they respond positively to in order to revise and refine your communications.

Having Unrealistic Expectations of Market Research

Another major pitfall that we've observed concerns having unrealistic expectations of market research. Some organizations expect market research to be the great panacea. Occasionally I get RFPs (requests for proposals) in which companies state that they want a research study that will: 1) provide the foundation for all their marketing efforts, 2) identify new products and services to launch this year, and 3) give them input for all their communications. I'm being somewhat facetious, but not entirely. Organizations want to maximize their research dollars by cramming as much as they can into one study. This goal is misguided. The result of this type of RFP is research that covers many, many things superficially.

One market-research project would be insufficient to achieve one of the objectives above. We could not identify all the new products and services that should be launched this year with one study. Instead, we would conduct several studies and use a variety of methods. First, we would do qualitative research to understand how current products are viewed and to identify the unmet needs that consumers have in this category. Once we've identified these unmet needs, we would create several product concepts and use qualitative research to get reactions to them and to refine them. The final product concepts would then be tested quantitatively to estimate potential customer demand and to determine the appropriate prices. The results would be used to launch new products or services for the organization.

Assuming Software is Smarter than Human Researchers

The last major pitfall we've seen in the last few years is the belief that software is somehow smarter and less biased than human researchers. We've seen this occur in the area of emotion detection where purveyors of facial expression software claim that their product can quickly and accurately analyze the reactions of respondents to products, services, and communications. We've compared many of the current software products that are available against a human being's analysis of emotion and we've been wildly disappointed in how poorly the software performs. And as my friend Daryl Travis of BrandTrust says: "It's hard enough for a person to decode another person, forget about software being able to do that."

Other products that purport to understand the human mind using neural imaging—some in the emotions space have been similarly disappointing. They provide pretty pictures of what's happening in the brain but often aren't clear as to what they're exactly measuring. We've seen similar issues with AI (Artificial Intelligence) and the notion that AI can be better than a human analytical mind. Because the software "learns" how to do the job better over time, people see it as superior to a human who learns. However, it's not clear what type of learning is happening exactly. We've found that these applications are eventually reliant on a human to interpret and use their findings intelligently.

I've had numerous market-research buyers tell me that they've invested in these types of products and have been extremely disappointed. At the end of the day, it's not as foolproof as they expected, not as brilliant as they had anticipated, and it doesn't replace a smart researcher who really understands human beings and what drives behavior.

CONCLUSION

In this book, I've talked about the strategic market-research approach and the impact it has on organizations. This approach is used at every stage of a research project. It all begins when we think about a strategic question(s) for an organization. At this point, we ask:

- What is the overarching question that the organization needs to answer?
- What are the specific questions that need to be addressed in order to answer this overarching question?
- What are the current hypotheses about the answer to this question?
- What actions will the organization take as a result of knowing this information?

Once we know the answers to these questions, we can design the research project and select the appropriate data-collection methods. Qualitative methods are appropriate at the beginning of a project for understanding the many thoughts, feelings, and behaviors of a group of people. We then use quantitative research to measure the things that we unearthed in qualitative work and to test our hypotheses. The specific qualitative and quantitative techniques we use depend on the objectives of our project and the tradeoffs we need to make for the study.

Now the real work begins as we delve into our project and try to get the depth we need to answer the strategic question. There are numerous ways to gain insight through qualitative research. One way is to hear more than just what respondents are saying, and another way is to ask the same questions in several different ways to understand the parameters of an answer. Other ways of getting a deep understanding involve probing, testing specific hypotheses, and testing potential scenarios. In general, the goal of qualitative research is to have a different discussion in the last focus group or interview than in the first one. Over time, you will gain a deeper understanding of the issue and will understand it in a different way. Obtaining depth in quantitative research involves some of the same techniques used in qualitative work, such as testing hypotheses and scenarios, but it also involves using skip patterns and exploring issues in detail with specific groups of respondents. It also involves using open-ended response categories and questions.

One way that we go beyond what respondents tell us in qualitative work is to read the nonverbal communications of research respondents. The method that I developed is PERCEIVE™. Each letter stands for a major piece of nonverbal communication. *P* stands for proximity, *E* is for expressions, *R* is for relative orientation, *C* is for contact (physical touching), *E* is for eyes, *I* is for individual gestures, *V* is for voice, and *E* stands for existence of adaptors, which are those small, fidgety behaviors that people do when they're stressed or bored. The sum of all these areas of nonverbal communication speaks volumes. When watching a person, I adhere to three rules: 1) watch for individual variations from his or her baseline; 2) watch for variations from the normal situation; and 3) watch for variations expressed toward different people.

Another way of obtaining insight in research projects is to understand the role that emotions play in how people view brands, products, and services. There are several ways that we delve into the emotional lives of our respondents. Before using any specific techniques, we create an atmosphere of comfort and trust, and we respond to people respectfully and with understanding when they express themselves. We also use a variety of techniques such as projection exercises, word associations, collages, stories, and salient memories. We also talk to respondents about their hopes and dreams to understand what role products and services play in their lives.

As our project evolves into quantitative research, we design our surveys to leverage all of the qualitative work we've done up to this point. We analyze numeric data to understand what drives markets. Our goal is to test our hypotheses and to answer specific questions. We use a variety of research designs and statistical analyses to help us. We query our data and test our hypotheses, leading to other questions and further analyses. By approaching our data analysis in this way, we understand what drives a market.

At the end of the road, we interpret the results and make strategic recommendations for an organization. Unfortunately, just repeating the data to the client is not the answer. Interpreting research results is not just about selecting the concept with the highest score or with the greatest percentage of respondents who liked it. It's about looking more deeply into the research results and asking several questions. What are respondents really saying when they give something a high score? The evaluation criteria that consumers use may be different than the ones we use to help an organization. We assess what consumers are telling us, and then what makes sense for a company. For example, when testing a new product, we consider how well this product fits with the brand, how well the company could execute it, and what the company would need to support its launch.

If you conduct, buy, or use market research, I encourage you to use the strategic approach. It will make the difference between collections of data and findings that inspire and change organizations. Good luck in your future research endeavors!

REFERENCES

Banse, R., & Scherer, K. R. (1996). Acoustic profiles in vocal emotion expression. Journal of Personality and Social Psychology, 70, 614–36.

Beall, A. E. (2007). Can a new smile make you look more intelligent and successful? The Dental Clinics of North America, 51 (2), 289–97.

Bechara, A. (2004). The role of emotion in decision-making: Evidence from neurological patients with orbitofrontal damage. Brain and Cognition, 55, 30–40.

Bowers, D., & Brereton, M. (2017). The AMA gold report 2017 top 50 market research firms. AMA Organization Publications. Available online: https://www.ama.org/publications/MarketingNews/Pages/the-ama-gold-report-2017-top-50-market-research-firms.aspx

Dovidio, J. F., Kawakami, K., Johnson, C., Johnson, B, & Howard, A. (1997). On the nature of prejudice: Automatic and controlled processes. Journal of Experimental Social Psychology, 33, 510–40.

Campbell, W. K., & Sedikides, C. (1999). Self-threat magnifies the self-serving bias: A meta-analytic integration. Review of General Psychology, 3, 23–43.

Ekman, P. (2003). Emotions Revealed. New York: Times Books.

Ekman, P., & Friesen, W. V. (1975). Unmasking the Face: A Guide to Recognizing Emotions From Facial Clues. Englewood Cliffs, NJ: Prentice-Hall

Kahneman, D. (2013). Thinking fast and slow. New York: Farrar, Straus and Giroux

Levinger, G. (1983). Development and change. Chapter 8 in H. H. Kelley et al., Close Relationships. San Francisco: Freeman, 1983.

Maestripier, D., Schino, G., Aureli, F. & Troisi, A. (1992). A modest proposal: Displacement activities as an indicator of emotions in primates. Animal Behavior, 44, 967–79.

MSN Money (2014). Stock Chart. Retrieved April 15, 2014, from http://on-msn.com/1euRbss

Myers, D. G. (2002). Social Psychology, 7th Edition. New York: McGraw Hill.

Pennebaker, J. W. (2011). The Secret Life of Pronouns. New York: Bloomsbury Press.

Pew Research Center (2018). Mobile Fact Sheet. Available online: http://www.pewinternet.org/fact-sheet/mobile/

Pittam, J., & Scherer, K. R. (1993). Vocal expression and communication of emotion. In M. Lewis & J. Haviland (Eds.), The Handbook of Emotion (pp. 185–97). New York: Guilford Press.

Remland, M. S. (2000). Nonverbal Communication in Everyday Life. Boston: Houghton Mifflin Company.

Richter, F. (2018). Landline phones are a dying breed. Statista.com. Available online: https://www.statista.com/chart/2072/landline-phones-in-the-united-states/

Weinstein, N. D. (1980) Unrealistic optimism about future life events. Journal of Personality and Social Psychology, 39, 806–20.

ANNE E. BEALL, PH.D.

Anne E. Beall is the founder and CEO of Beall Research, Inc. She specializes in strategic market research and was previously at The Boston Consulting Group (BCG). During her tenure at BCG, Beall directed market research for the Chicago office. She specializes in leveraging frameworks and concepts from psychology to market research and has particular expertise in the area of emotions.

Beall conducts both qualitative and quantitative market research. She specializes in conducting large-scale, complex strategic studies for Fortune 500 companies. She has conducted research on brand positioning and brand equity, determinants of customer loyalty and switching behavior, development of new product concepts, extendibility of brands, launches of new products and services, pricing, and segmentations of consumers and businesses. She has worked in a variety of industries, including food, beverages, telecommunications, insurance, brokerage firms, utilities, package transportation and delivery, retail, schools, hospitals, foundations, furniture, and personal-care products.

Beall has conducted hundreds of in-depth interviews, focus groups and surveys across many industries. She specializes in analyzing what respondents say and, more important, what they don't say. She has an unusual sensitivity for people and has created a method for reading nonverbal behavior called PERCEIVE™, which can be used to read respondents when they are unable or unwilling to express their thoughts and feelings.

Beall has written book chapters and articles about consumer psychology and marketing. She has published the following books: *Cinderella Didn't Live Happily Ever After: The Hidden Message in Fairy Tales*, *Heartfelt Connections: How Animals & People Help One Another*, *Community Cats: A Journal Into the World of Feral Cats*, *Reading the Hidden Communications around You: A Guide to Reding Body Language in the Workplace*.

Beall received her MS, MPhil, and PhD degrees in social psychology from Yale University. In her spare time she runs, fosters stray cats for various shelters in Chicago, and enjoys the many restaurants of the city.

Also by Anne E. Beall

Reading the Hidden Communications Around You: A Guide to Reading the Body Language of Customers and Colleagues
Reading Hidden Communications

5-Minute Sleep Meditations: Fantasy Journeys with an Inspirational Message
5-Minute Sleep Meditations

5-Minute Meditation Vacations: Magical Journeys with a Personal Message
5-Minute Meditation Vacations

Words of Encouragement: Inspirational Quotes and Profiles to Cultivate Strength
Words of Encouragement

Heartfelt Connections: How Animals and People Help One Another
Heartfelt Connections

Community Cats: A Journey Into the World of Feral Cats
Community Cats

Heroic Helpful and Caring Cats: Felines Who Make a Difference
Heroic, Helpful & Caring Cats

Cinderella Didn't Live Happily Ever After: The Hidden Messages in Fairy Tales
Cinderella Didn't Live Happily Ever After

The Psychology of Gender
Psychology of Gender

Made in United States
North Haven, CT
21 August 2022

22996361R00075